SINGAPORE WOMEN'S CHARTER

The **Institute of Southeast Asian Studies (ISEAS)** was established as an autonomous organization in 1968. It is a regional centre dedicated to the study of socio-political, security and economic trends and developments in Southeast Asia and its wider geostrategic and economic environment. The Institute's research programmes are the Regional Economic Studies (RES, including ASEAN and APEC), Regional Strategic and Political Studies (RSPS), and Regional Social and Cultural Studies (RSCS).

ISEAS Publishing, an established academic press, has issued more than 2,000 books and journals. It is the largest scholarly publisher of research about Southeast Asia from within the region. ISEAS Publishing works with many other academic and trade publishers and distributors to disseminate important research and analyses from and about Southeast Asia to the rest of the world.

SINGAPORE WOMEN'S CHARTER

Roles, Responsibilities and Rights in Marriage

EDITED BY

THERESA W. DEVASAHAYAM

ISEAS

INSTITUTE OF SOUTHEAST ASIAN STUDIES
Singapore

First published in Singapore in 2011 by ISEAS Publishing
Institute of Southeast Asian Studies
30 Heng Mui Keng Terrace
Pasir Panjang
Singapore 119614

E-mail: publish@iseas.edu.sg
Website: http://bookshop.iseas.edu.sg

ISEAS would like to express gratitude to Konrad Ardenauer Stiftung (KAS) for making the symposium as well as this publication possible.

The responsibility for facts and opinions in this publication rests exclusively with the authors and their interpretations do not necessarily reflect the views or the policy of the publisher or its supporters.

ISEAS Library Cataloguing-in-Publication Data

Singapore Women's Charter : roles, responsibilities and rights in
    marriage / edited by Theresa W. Devasahayam.
    1. Women's rights—Singapore.
    2. Women—Legal status, laws, etc.—Singapore.
    I. Devasahayam, Theresa W.
HQ1236.5 S6D48   2011

ISBN 978-981-4279-76-5 (soft cover)
ISBN 978-981-4345-01-9 (hard cover)
ISBN 978-981-4279-75-8 (E-book PDF)

Typeset by International Typesetters Pte Ltd
Printed in Singapore by Utopia Press Pte Ltd

Contents

Contributors

Theresa W. Devasahayam, Gender Studies Programme coordinator, Institute of Southeast Asian Studies

Ellen Lee, Family Law specialist and member of parliament, Singapore

Leong Wai Kum, professor, Faculty of Law, National University of Singapore

Sudha Nair, assistant professor, Department of Social Work, National University of Singapore

Kanwaljit Soin, consultant orthopaedic surgeon and social activist, Singapore

Ann Wee, associate professorial fellow, Department of Social Work, National University of Singapore

Foreword

I thank the Director of the Institute of Southeast Asian Studies (ISEAS), Ambassador K. Kesavapany, for inviting me to contribute the Foreword to this volume which contains the papers submitted to the symposium "Revisiting the Singapore Women's Charter". The symposium was organized by Dr Theresa W. Devasahayam, the coordinator of the gender studies programme at ISEAS.

First, I am very pleased that ISEAS has a programme on gender policies and issues in Southeast Asia. I consider the emancipation of women and the recognition that women are entitled to equal rights with men as one of the greatest achievements of the twentieth century. The UN Convention on the Elimination of All Forms of Discrimination Against Women (CEDAW), of which Singapore is a party, is one of the most important treaties in public international law. It seeks to put an end to a shameful period in human history, lasting thousands of years, during which women were treated as chattels and having no rights or as inferior human beings and discriminated against in a myriad of ways. It is, of course, true that CEDAW has not been fully implemented by all the state parties or by all the member states of the UN. However, those who invoke culture or religion to justify discrimination against women know that theirs is a losing battle. They are on the wrong side of history.

I am convinced that one day, in this century, the dream that women will enjoy the same rights as men will come true for all womenkind.

Second, in Singapore the enactment of the Women's Charter in 1961 was a revolutionary act. It put an end to polygamy for all Singaporeans, except for Muslims. Section 46 of the Charter, *inter alia*, gives the wife the right to use her surname and name; to have equal rights with her husband in running the matrimonial household; and the right to engage in any trade or profession or social activities. Compared to the situation prior to 1961, these were transformative propositions. A member of the Singapore Legislative Assembly was right when he described the Women's Charter as a bill of rights for Singapore women. There is a disagreement in this book between Dr Kanwaljit Soin and Professor Leong Wai Kum on whether the title of the legislation, "Women's Charter", should be retained or changed to "Family Charter". I agree with Professor Leong that, for historical reasons, it is better to retain the name. I agree with her that it would be unfortunate if future generations of Singaporeans, especially women, were to forget the struggles of women over many decades which eventually led to the enactment of this landmark legislation.

Third, I am disappointed to learn from the book that divorce has been on the rise looking at marriage trends in the past decade and more. The Ministry of Community Development, Youth and Sports (MCYS) has been campaigning to encourage young Singaporeans to marry and to have children. I think MCYS should also focus on why such a high percentage of our marriages break down and, whether, when children are involved, there is anything which our counsellors can do to prevent the dissolution of such marriages. I am also appalled to read accounts of the shabby treatment given to children in families which have broken down because of domestic violence. If the father is violent and harms his family, why should the law require the victimized child to undergo counselling? There is obviously also a need to re-think the existing law and practice regarding the treatment of an erring husband who refuses to pay maintenance. Why is there a hesitation to apply to the court to impose attachment? The law should also be amended to allow a member of the victim's family to apply to court for a protective order. The victim may be too fearful or traumatized to do so.

Conclusion

Singapore has come a long way since the Women's Charter came into force in 1962. Women have attained equality with men in education at all levels. Women have also achieved equality with men in employment. Some discriminatory practices, such as the quota on women in the medical school, have been swept away. However, the discrimination against female civil servants, regarding the entitlement of their family members to medical benefits, has not been fully abolished. The principle of equal pay for equal work is part of our norms and practices. We have many female chief executive officers, several female permanent secretaries in our civil service and one female minister. There are still too few women in our parliament and on our boards and in decision-making positions in both our public and private sectors. However, the march of our women towards full equality is an unstoppable one. The progress of Singapore has benefited enormously from the contributions of our educated and empowered women. Let us break every remaining glass ceiling impeding the rise of women to the top in Singapore.

Professor Tommy Koh
Chairman
Centre for International Law
National University of Singapore

Keynote Address "Women's Charter to Family Charter"

Dr Kanwaljit Soin
ISEAS Symposium
"Revisiting the Singapore Women's Charter"
10 June 2009

Introduction

I feel very privileged to be given this honour as I see so many distinguished people in the audience who are more qualified than me to fill this role. Nevertheless, I must confess that I readily accepted the invitation when I was asked as this sort of an opportunity seldom comes my way. Now that I am standing here, I am shamelessly going to take advantage of my position. Instead of an overview as might be expected of me, I am only going to speak on issues that I have some knowledge of and am passionate about. This means that I am going to leave the field wide open to the other speakers whom I think are really the substantive part of the forum and whom I salute as the real experts.

Enactment of the Charter — 1961

The PAP government enacted the Women's Charter as part of an election promise in 1959. At the second reading of the

Women's Charter Bill in 1960, Minister K.M. Byrne revealed that the statute really proposed to regulate the formation of marriage and family life, but had been given the grandiose name of the "Women's Charter" because the bill was making a very great change in the personal lives of many women. We must remember that at that time polygamy was the order of the day and the bill was primarily aimed at legislating monogamy for all non-Muslims. The Women's Charter took effect on 15 September 1961. It ensured equal rights for married women *vis-à-vis* their husbands. In the early 1960s, this legislation was ahead of its time in promulgating the idea of marriage as an "equal cooperative partnership of different efforts".

Shortcomings — The Need For A Family Charter

In 2011, the Women's Charter will see its golden anniversary, an age when some things need a makeover. At present, many people think that the Women's Charter is not an appropriate name for this legislation as it does not reflect the spirit of the legislation. The name gives the impression that men are being denied something that is reserved only for women. The Women's Charter actually deals with family law. This becomes even more obvious when we look at the amendments to the Women's Charter in 1996 — those dealing with family violence, including elder abuse, and the marriage of transsexuals. Do these concern only women? Of course not. They concern the family. Therefore, what we should do is incorporate the present Women's Charter and other legislation dealing with the family, for example, the Maintenance of Parents Act, and make it one big piece of legislation and call it the "Family Charter". However, we will first have to remove Part XI from the Women's Charter because this section deals mainly with offences relating to prostitution and, therefore, rightfully belongs to the Penal Code.

I would like to suggest that in drafting this new "Family Charter", we should include the five core family values that have been accepted as ideals by us in Singapore. Thus, the Family Charter will not only be the law to regulate family relationships and behaviour, but will also promote values and beliefs that we hold dear. We should draft the legislation in ordinary understandable English and translate it into all the official languages so that it becomes familiar to all of us.

Amendments to Women's Charter 1996

The Women's Charter has undergone various amendments in the last fifty years and these were especially significant in 1996. There were four main areas that were affected:

(i) Protection of family members from violence;
(ii) Maintenance of wife and children and enforcement of maintenance orders;
(iii) Division of matrimonial assets on termination of marriage; and,
(iv) Marriage for persons who have undergone sex reassignment surgery.

Protection From Family Violence

I will only touch on two of these areas — family violence and maintenance. I moved a Family Violence Bill when I was in parliament in November 1995. Unfortunately, the bill was defeated, but some good things did come about from this aborted bill. Firstly, it generated a great deal of media attention and this brought the subject of family violence very much into the public consciousness. Here I have to acknowledge with pride that it was entirely due to AWARE (Association of Women for Action and Research) and my association with it as a founder member and then as President of AWARE (1991–93), that I was sensitized to the issue of family violence. AWARE has a long history of doing research and advocacy on domestic violence and deserves a lot of credit for bringing this issue to the forefront.

Secondly, some important legislative and practice changes were implemented as a result of the Family Violence Bill. At the second reading of the bill on 1 November 1995, Mr Wong Kan Seng (at that time Minister for Home Affairs) said the following:

> Since April last year, an interagency Work Group on Spousal Violence was formed by my Ministry to recommend measures to improve and co-ordinate the management of spousal violence cases and to find innovative ways of dealing with them. Here I would give credit to Dr Soin for the impetus in setting up this Work Group ...

After the bill was defeated, the Women's Charter (Amendment) Bill was moved in May 1996 and sent to a Select Committee and finally the amendments were passed in Parliament in August 1996. Many of the provisions of the Family Violence Bill were incorporated into the amended Women's Charter 1996.

Comparison: Women's Charter and the Family Violence Bill

So at this juncture, I would like to compare the aborted bill with the amended Women's Charter in four areas that I think fall short in the Women's Charter.

(i) *The range of persons protected in the amended Women's Charter:* As in the Family Violence Bill, this includes spouse, former spouse, child, stepchild, adopted child, parents, parents-in-law, and any other relative or incapacitated person who is regarded by the court as a member of the family. However, unmarried couples who are living together are excluded. The message appears to be that if they are not married, they do not deserve to be protected. The solution proposed by the Family Violence Bill would have allowed the courts to consider even *de facto* or what lawyers call common law husbands and wives, and not exclude them altogether as is now the case in the Women's Charter. However, such relations outside registered marriages are subtly on the increase and sometimes reach parenthood status. The illegitimate status of the couple, if you want to call it that, is not the issue here — protection from an abusive relationship is the issue and this is not recognized under the Charter.

(ii) *The person who may apply for a Protection Order*: In the amended Women's Charter where violence between spouses is concerned, only the victim can apply for a protection order. This provision has not taken into account that in cases of spousal violence, the victim often believes that she cannot help herself, and often fails to take any action to end the abusive relationship because of this sense of learned helplessness. Those who work in the area of domestic violence are well aware of this syndrome. Therefore in the Family Violence Bill, the relevant provision states that any person who has reason to believe that family violence (including spousal violence) is being committed or has been committed, can inform an enforcement officer who will then provide assistance to the victim and can even apply for a protection order for her. This is also the legislation in various Australian states.

(iii) *Type of harm to be prevented*: In the Family Violence Bill, it is an offence to "compel a family member by force to engage in any sexual act or misconduct", but in the amended Women's Charter this has been omitted. Representations by AWARE and the Association of Women Lawyers were made at the Select Committee hearing of the Women's Charter in 1996 to include unconsented sexual acts or conduct in the definition of family violence, but these were rejected. This means that at present, a forced sexual act or misconduct by an abuser on a family member can only come under the provision of the Penal Code or the Children and Young Persons Act. This process is difficult and complicated. Let me give you an example — if a brother is molesting his sister, then the family may not be averse to the sister applying for a protection order and the brother being sent for mandatory counselling. In this scenario, there will be no criminal record for the brother. However, if the Penal Code were to be invoked, then the process becomes adversarial and lengthy, and the family may stop the sister from taking any action for fear of shameful publicity and that the brother may end up with a criminal record. If a forced sexual act or misconduct between spouses or family members was recognized as an offence in the amended Women's Charter as it was in the Family Violence Bill, then a clear message would be sent to all family members and spouses that this type of conduct is not just a private matter, but a violation of a person's body, and family members can resort to protection orders. This procedure is more conducive to the victim making a report in the hope of ending the violence, than leaving it to legislation in the Penal Code because the victim and family concerned often avoid this route.

(iv) *Counselling*: In the amended Women's Charter, mandatory counselling can be imposed not only on the abuser, but also on the victim and her children, while in the Family Violence Bill, mandatory counselling is reserved only for the abuser. I feel that the victim can be offered voluntary support and counselling, but to make it mandatory sends a wrong message to the abuser — he may interpret this as the victim is also at fault as both get mandatory counselling.

Removing Discrimination: Need for Maintenance of Husband

I will now turn to the issue of maintenance of husbands. When the Women's Charter was first passed in 1961, it was hailed as a very progressive piece of legislation mainly because of the way the rights and duties of the husband and wife were framed. I shall read Section 46 to refresh our memories:

(i) Upon the solemnization of marriage, the husband and wife shall be mutually bound to cooperate with each other in safeguarding the interests of the union and in caring and providing for the children.
(ii) The husband and the wife shall have the right separately to engage in any trade and profession or in social activities.
(iii) The wife shall have the right to use her own surname and name separately.
(iv) The husband and wife shall have equal rights in the running of the matrimonial household.

Thus as far back as 1961, the Women's Charter clearly propounded the idea of marriage as an equal partnership between a man and a woman. Yet nearly fifty years later, Section 69 of the Charter grants only the wife the right to claim maintenance from her husband and not the other way around. Here I would like to quote Professor Leong Wai Kum on the subject of maintenance:

> A wife does not owe a similar obligation and can ignore the subsistence needs of her husband even if she were fully capable of meeting them. This cannot

be right. So while this obligation is not likely to be
enforced often, it should be part of the law.

I completely agree with this view. It is only fair and equitable
that a wife should maintain her husband if this is necessary.
Many wives nowadays earn as much and even more than
their husbands. In this era, maintenance should be on the
basis of need and not on the basis of sex. Some men may
not be able to find work or may be incapacitated by a
chronic illness. If an ex-husband develops chronic kidney
failure and cannot work, should an ex-wife who is a high
earner be absolved from supporting him while the financial
burden fall on other family members or the community and
the taxpayer? If this woman does not voluntarily want to
support her ill ex-husband, why should she get away scot-
free and not shoulder her rightful responsibility stemming
from the former union?

The unilateral character of maintenance where only
husbands maintain wives was inherited from common
law because in bygone times a married woman lost her
capacity to own property when she married her husband
who would then automatically own her property. Therefore
to compensate the woman for this loss, the husband had
to maintain her. As this practice no longer holds, we have
to change the legislation so that we will have mutual
maintenance and this will reflect the guiding principle of
the Women's Charter that marriage is an "equal cooperative
partnership of different efforts".

The existing anomaly violates the spirit of the Charter
and puts women in a difficult position. It allows some men
to articulate that women cannot ask for equal rights if they
do not want to shoulder equal responsibilities in matters

such as maintenance. In this provision if we simply change the word "wife" to "spouse", we will dispel the belief that the Charter discriminates against men. During the Select Committee hearing in 1996, five women representing women's groups expressed the view that maintenance to husbands, especially in appropriate cases, should be allowed, but unfortunately this plea failed.

Here, I would like to quote the then Acting Minister for Community Development's reply when I raised this matter of maintenance for husbands in May 1996 in parliament. This was part of his reply:

> As for allowing maintenance for husbands, I am of the view that existing provisions of allowing only women to claim for maintenance should be maintained, at least for the present. Call me old-fashioned if you will; call me a male chauvinist if you must, but my upbringing and my background tell me that it is the duty of the husband to maintain the wife. And I think I speak for most, if not all, the husbands of this House.

I am afraid that the Minister was not spared a rebuttal in parliament for expressing this view. This is what I had to say in reply, which had to be framed as a point of clarification to fit in with the rules of parliamentary procedure:

> I respect the Minister's view. He wants to be old-fashioned or male chauvinist. But I would like to clarify that when we are making a public policy we will have to leave aside our personal feelings and look at what the social context is. So I would like the Minister to clarify this point about maintenance in view of the statistics that I quoted that [show] many women are marrying downwards now and earning as

much as [their husbands], if not more. In that type of a social milieu, Sir, would the Minister reconsider that husbands can be entitled to maintenance under appropriate circumstances because in the end it is the welfare of the family that may be compromised if in appropriate circumstances we do not award maintenance to the husband?

Unfortunately, even this repeat plea did not move the Minister to change his mind. Maynard Keynes had this to say once and it applies aptly to the occasion at hand: "When circumstances change, I change my view. What do you do, Sir?"

In these days of financial upheaval where husbands have lost jobs and the wife continues to be fruitfully employed, it is necessary to have in place a reassuring law that does not make a husband destitute. There is, therefore, a need for a complete change of heart and mind towards this issue of mutual maintenance. To come back to Keynes again who was ruthless in discarding ideas (including his own) if they failed to act as a guide to change circumstances: "The difficulty lies not so much in developing new ideas", he argued, "as in escaping old ones." The Women's Charter started out being a progressive piece of legislation. We should not now allow it to stagnate.

I would like to make a further point. It is interesting to note that in India a provision for maintenance exists in all matrimonial laws, with the difference that under the Hindu Marriage Act, either party — wife or husband — can claim maintenance, while under the Muslim Personal Law or the Indian Christian Marriage Act, it is only the wife who can claim maintenance.

Constitutional Issue

There have been some local legal thinkers who have questioned whether the provision in the Women's Charter regarding maintenance being available only to women and not to men violates Article 12(1) of the Constitution of the Republic of Singapore, which provides that "all persons are equal before the law and entitled to the equal protection of the law". It will be interesting if the constitutionality of this maintenance provision is brought before the Supreme Court to be tested.

Conclusion

Here I am going to quote Professor Leong Wai Kum once more, who, in my opinion, is the foremost expert on marriage and family law: "We respect a family law more when it mirrors our lives and hopes."

I end on this note in the hope that this is the direction that family law will continue to take in Singapore.

References

Chan Wing Cheong. "Latest Improvements to the Women's Charter". *Singapore Journal of Legal Studies* (1996): 553–99.

Low, Kelvin Fatt-Kin, Kelry Loi Chit Fai, and Serene Wee Ai Yin. "Towards a Maintenance of Equality (Part I): A Study of the Constitutionality of Maintenance Provisions that Sexually Discriminate". *Singapore Law Review* 19 (1998): 45–76.

Parliamentary Reports 2-5-1996, columns 95, 96.

1
Legal Mechanisms for Protecting Women's Rights: Examples from Southeast Asia

Theresa W. Devasahayam

Introduction

With increasing levels of economic development in countries across the world, the assumption is that there would be greater equality between men and women in every facet of life. It is no longer a surprise to see women making a mark in the public sphere: there are women in high-level positions in government, the private sector, including banking and financial services, international organizations, and others. But women would not have come thus far without the endorsement of the state through the installation of laws and policies engendering equality between the sexes. Most countries have in place national laws to protect women's rights, in addition to having ratified the most distinct international human rights instrument related to women — the UN Convention on the Elimination of All Forms of Discrimination Against Women

(CEDAW). Others have complemented their legislation and their support of CEDAW with targeted programmes to eliminate any discrimination against women.

In spite of these efforts, there have been mixed findings reported on women's advancement in many countries across the world — whether it is in education, employment, health, or matters in the private domain such as domestic violence.[1] For example, "violence against women and sexual exploitation remain serious problems ...", according to a CEDAW report.[2] Only eighty-nine member states of the United Nations have legislative provisions for addressing domestic violence as of 2006 and, of this number, sixty states have specific domestic violence laws while others have mapped out clear national plans on this issue.[3] Clearly, not all governments have conscientiously installed the relevant legislation to protect women, drawing criticisms from some human rights quarters which accuse "[some] governments [of] not living up to their promises ...".[4] In response, these governments have evoked the "separate sphere ideology", maintaining that some issues are related to the private domain in which governments should not interfere (Mertus 1995, p. 135). But if governments do recognize that "disrupt[ing] existing family arrangements and influenc[ing] women's ability to participate fully in the social and political spheres" through legal provisions results in protecting women's rights (Mertus 1995, p. 135), this may have the effect of fulfilling larger economic, political, and social goals.

In spite of recognizing that the law is "a powerful weapon in the struggle for social, political and economic equality between men and women ... the struggle to produce a society where sex is no longer a barrier to equality" continues to be prevalent in many countries (Mezey 2001, p. 420). While installing legal provisions to protect women's rights in the private domain as well as in other areas impeding gender equality is a critical step forward for women's empowerment, it must be noted that having laws in place does not always guarantee that women's rights are protected. It has been found that various obstacles exist in the implementation of these laws, together with the problem that these laws have shortcomings which, in turn, have perpetuated and reinforced gender inequality instead. It must also be recognized that national laws are not applied in isolation. Rather these laws protecting women's rights are often operating in tandem with religious laws and cultural norms, sometimes resulting in clashes (cf. Mertus 1995). For example, it has been found in the region that men continue to have "the unilateral right ... to repudiate his wife, contract polygamous marriages, claim conjugal rights ..." based on religious laws, posing problems in developing a model of equality for both men and women (Economic and Social Commission for Asia and the Pacific 1997, p. 34).[5] Thus in many instances, the implementation of national laws protecting women is obstructed by a myriad of variables — each having the effect of suppressing or hindering gender equality or even reproducing gender inequality. For these reasons, in spite of the existence of national laws protecting women's rights in many areas, women continue to be disadvantaged.

The Fight for Women's Rights: A Woman's Story

National laws protecting women's rights in Southeast Asia run the gamut. There are laws in existence to protect women's rights in a range of contexts — marriage, divorce, and domestic violence to name a few. While laws are in existence to protect women's rights in most countries in Southeast Asia, family or marriage law — argued to be a significant indicator of women's status (Asian Development Bank 2002), presumably because of how it shapes women's private lives — stands out as one of several legislative protections. But many countries have other complementary laws to protect women's rights in a marriage. The enactment of a law on domestic violence is one such example. A look at the development of these laws in three countries in Southeast Asia — Indonesia, Malaysia, and Thailand — displays a fascinating pattern. In each country, women collectively have played an intrinsic role in protecting their rights in marriage, whether by contesting, reforming, or promulgating the existing laws. But in many cases, their success has only been partial. The histories of women activists suggest that one reason for their partial success might have been because they did not campaign with one voice; rather there were different groups of women activists, each with its own vision of how to address gender inequality. Another could be that women activists' understanding of "rights" is a "project-in-process, being constantly rescrutinized, reframed and reworked" (Stivens 2003, p. 136), albeit marked by a rich past going back at least to colonial times.

Indonesia is a case in point with its Marriage Law promulgated in 1974. But it took more than sixty years of lobbying on the part of women's organizations to bring this law in force (Robinson 2006). Women were determined in protecting their rights in the years before independence: "Public debates about religion and law have been inextricably bound with demands by women's groups that the state extend its grasp into the private domain of the family" (Robinson 2006, p. 187). These women's groups were adamant about improving their well-being, especially with regards to marriage and divorce. In particular, the issues that fuelled their campaigns were child marriage, forced marriage, polygamous marriage outside the parameters outlined by Islam, arbitrary divorce by husbands, and the absence of a requirement to enforce the payment of alimony.

Butt (1999) notes that the *Kongres Perempuan Indonesia* (Indonesian Women's Congress), a conglomeration of prominent women's organizations from across the country, aggressively campaigned to improve the rights of women in marriage in pre-independent Indonesia. About thirty women's groups gathered in 1928 to take up the issues of polygamy, forced and underage marriage (Robinson 2006). The congress met several times again until 1935 when the Commission to Investigate Marriage Law was established. This was followed by a draft set of rules for the regulation of marriage among Muslims, which was set out to the women's congress. But conservative Islamic factions rejected the draft, although the issue of polygamy was not raised.

Katz and Katz (1975, as cited in Butt 1999) detail how the women's emancipation movement was closely allied to the independence movement. While resistance movements were active in ensuring that Indonesia did not return to the Dutch forces, women's organizations were concurrently advocating "woman-friendly legal instruments in the new state" (Robinson 2006, p. 192). The Indonesian Constitution was a clear representation of the culmination of the efforts of these women's organizations. Indonesian women were now equal to men in the eyes of the law with respect to marriage, education, economics, and culture. Law No. 22 of 1964 Concerning Registration of Marriages, Reconciliation and Divorce was issued. Under this law, failing to register a marriage incurred a fine. But the fight for the removal of polygamy and equal rights in divorce was far from over.

It was only with President Soeharto that the issue of a marriage reform law was resurrected. In 1973, a Matrimonial Bill was presented in parliament. It was this bill that ensured equal rights for women in marriage and divorce. Although generally supported by women's groups, the bill attracted criticisms from conservative religious elements as they argued that the bill contradicted Islamic law. The bill finally gave way to the promulgation of the Marriage Law on 2 January 1974.

Before the Marriage Law came into effect, Indonesian (Muslim) women were bound by the Islamic marriage law, although it has been argued that its adoption has been uneven across the country (Robinson 2006). Largely uncodified, this law left women with very few rights in marriage. Furthermore, men could take another wife without the consent of his first wife or existing wives. Divorce also came easier for a man while a woman faced different obstacles in initiating a divorce except in extreme situations.

It is this point that riled Indonesian women activists. Many felt that Islamic law made it too easy for men to divorce their wives: with the mere utterance of the word *talaq*, a man can repudiate his wife and secure a divorce from her (Asian Development Bank 2002).

Not only did women stand to gain from the enactment of the Marriage Law in 1974, but the Indonesian Government also viewed this move as a positive step towards countering division and divisive elements in society presented not only by Islam, but also by local cultural traditions which favoured men (Robinson 2006). Generating a national law also meant "inject[ing] certainty and consistency into marriage law" aimed at "unifying Indonesia's differing *adat* (traditional) and religious marriage laws ..." (Butt 1999, p. 125). Most importantly, codification of a national law on marriage by the state reinforced "the government as the ultimate authority in the administration of marriage law and as the arbiter of its legitimacy" (Johns 1987, p. 217, as cited in Butt 1999, p. 125).

The government further strengthened its grip on the religious courts through the Law on Religious Justice (No. 7 of 1989). Later in accordance to a presidential instruction, the Compilation of Islamic Law (*Kompilasi Hukum*) was created in 1991. As a result, the religious courts had to make judgements on marriage and divorce based on the secular law and not the *fiqh* (laws pertaining to ritual, moral, and social obligations) (Robinson 2006). Some scholars have opined that it was the Compilation that brought to a large degree greater gender equality (Bowen n.d., as cited in Robinson 2006). By no means does this suggest that women activists agreed wholeheartedly with the basic legal protections in the Compilation for women. Many took issue with how the New Order regime narrowly defined women's role in the private domain, while denying recognition to women's contributions in the political and economic spheres. There was also unhappiness with how women were "objectified" in the government's family planning scheme (Chandrakirana and Chuzaifah 2005, p. 60).

Furthermore, the fight against polygamy was not over for these women activists because extremist Islamic groups at the close of the Soeharto regime in 1998 seized the opportunity to promote polygamy once again (Chandrakirana and Chuzaifah 2005). Many of these groups had large followings of women who "adopt[ed] strict Muslim dress codes and glorif[ied] women's domestic and reproductive roles" (Wieringa 2005, p. 7). In the face of this opposition, LBH-APIK (Indonesian Women's Association for Justice & Legal Aid Institute) continued to call for changes to the 1974 Marriage Law, arguing that polygamy led to devastating effects on marriage, such as domestic violence as well as other forms of psychological, sexual, and economic abuse. They pushed their cause further by asserting that polygamy was the most significant factor for divorce. Their fight for women's rights has been successful to the extent that they have been able to inspire other groups such as the umbrella organization, KOWANI, to follow in their path (Robinson 2006).

In September 2004, a working group for gender mainstreaming in the Department of Religious Affairs proposed an alternative draft on family law. The Counter Legal Draft (CLD) is based on six principles: human welfare (*al-maslahat*), gender equality and fairness (*al-musawah al-jinsiyyah*), pluralism (*al-tàaddudiyyah*), nationalism (*al-muwathanah*), human rights (*iqamat al-huquq al-insaniyyah*), and democracy (*al-dimuqratiyyah*). Based on these principles, the CLD proposes alternative reforms on various issues encompassing marriage and inheritances, more specifically, the definition of marriage, the role of the guardian as one of the obligatory require-ments of marriage, marriage registration, the minimum age of marriage for the bride, *mahar* (dowry), the rights and obligations of husband and wife, *nusyuz* (disobedience), interreligious marriage, the right to divorce and *ruju'* (legally remarry the wife from whom one had been divorced) for a wife, *'idda* (the waiting time for a wife wherein she is not allowed to remarry after being divorced or because of the death of her husband), *ihdad* (mourning period), and inheritance issues. In addition, the CLD proposes a complete ban on the practice of polygamy.

The assumption underlying the CLD is that the classical *fiqh* perspective on marriage as encapsulated in the Compilation of Islamic Law positions women as sexual objects in subordination to men. In contrast, the CLD offers a new paradigm on marriage that places women as equal law subjects to men and with equal rights. In short, marriage should be defined as a commitment voluntarily entered into by two equal parties.

The proponents of the CLD also maintain that the proposal fights domination, discrimination, exploitation, and violence in marriage. The aim is also to put a stop to forced marriages, juvenile marriages, informal marriages, unrecorded marriages, and polygamous marriages. The CLD is by no means the final formulation of marriage by all parties; instead the proposal should be seen as an *ijtihad* (effort) that promotes basic Islamic teachings on marriage.

Thailand shows remarkable similarity to the Indonesian context in the way women were able to draw public attention to the inequalities they faced. By and large, Thai law "formalized discrimination against women, legitimating male dominance over women in marriage, divorce, and allocation of marital property ..." (Peach 2006, p. 35). Polygamy was legal until 1935 and it was commonplace for men from the upper classes to have several wives. The man had the right to treat his wife/wives as private property, punishing her/them as he saw fit (and in some extreme cases, resorting to execution) in accordance with the Three Seals Law of 1805. This law also granted him the power to manage his wife's/wives' monies and the land which she/they had brought into the marriage. The Monogamy Act (1935), however, put a stop to the powers bestowed on men through the Three Seals Law. In spite of this progress, other gender inequalities in marriage remained for a few decades.

It was only in the late 1960s that a group of educated, affluent, and professional women from the legal and business sectors actively took to challenging the family law. This group of women was consumed with two issues: matrimonial property management and the prevention of double marital registration (Somswasdi 2005). They sought to fight for the reform of the family law by lobbying members of the judiciary and high-level government officials. But their lobbying efforts were felt mainly in academic institutions and professional associations. The impulse to act among these women stemmed from the fact that polygamy continued to be a prevalent problem: their husbands were taking on minor wives in spite of the Monogamy Act already in place, and infidelity was rife. According to legal scholar Virada Somswasdi (2005), the campaign was limited as it "did not touch on the problem of the patriarchal structure of society, nor did it link up with [the inequality felt by the] lower income, rural women or academics. Nonetheless, it broke the ground for campaigns on a broader range of issues [later on]. At the very least, the women's efforts bore fruit as they eventually won the right to marital property management" (Somswasdi 2005, n.p.).

The efforts of these women provided a catalyst for other women's movements fighting for women's rights. In the years to come, issues such as women's human rights, domestic violence, violence against women in trafficking and prostitution, marital rape, reproductive rights, abortion, and various sexual orientations were taken up by women activists (Somswasdi 2005).

Malaysian women were also at the forefront in campaigning for their own rights on various issues. Six years after independence, a non-governmental multiracial women's organization called the National Council of Women's Organisations (NCWO) was formed (Ng, Maznah and tan 2006). Although the issue of unequal pay spurred the galvanization of women members of NCWO, the efforts of the NCWO were especially critical on matters of family law. By the 1960s, the registration of marriages was made compulsory, but this by no means put an end to polygamy. If a man's religion (notably Islam) or customary law permitted polygamy, he could register other marriages in spite of his already being married.

Although cognizant of the fact that Muslim women also faced similar dilemmas, the NCWO decided on reforming the laws concerning non-Muslim women first. With persistent fervour from the NCWO, the Royal Commission for Marriage and Divorce for Non-Muslims was set up in 1970. This Commission was tasked to examine existing laws on marriage and divorce in relation to the United Nations Convention on Human Rights regarding consent to marriage, minimum age of marriage, and registration of marriages. Soon afterwards, the NCWO submitted a memorandum advocating monogamous marriages to the Royal Commission. Its argument was that "polygamous marriages have 'deleterious effects' on the family — not just financial but emotional, as well as the moral upbringing of children ... [and that] 'all marriages by customary rites should be abolished' and [replaced by] a homogenous system provided for the solemnisation, registration and dissolution of monogamous marriages" (Abidah 2004, p. 137). In fighting against polygamy, the NCWO memorandum recommended the registration of all marriages by a competent authority, full and free consent by the parties involved, and the duties of the couple in a marriage. On maintenance, the memorandum recommended that a married woman may apply to a district or magistrate's court for a monthly allowance in proportion to her husband's earnings. In relation to divorce, either party should have the right to petition for a divorce.

Based on the Law Reform (Marriage and Divorce) Bill 1972, the Law Reform (Marriage and Divorce) Act 1976, providing for monogamous marriages and consolidating the law on divorce, was passed. The Act which took effect in March 1981 was a watershed because for the first time, anyone practising polygamy could be prosecuted (see also Siraj 1994). More important, it was reiterated that especially for the lowly-educated women: "[the Act] gives greater protection to ... the under-privileged lower income and illiterate groups. It ensured that these women were not victimised by men who took advantage of customs permitting polygamy and often ignored their responsibilities" (Abidah 2004, p. 139).

Women activists in the NCWO also took issue with the Married Women and Children (Maintenance) Act 1950, and pushed for recommendations that the maintenance allowance allocated to women be aligned with current cost of living and that all maintenance should be binding and paid through the courts. NCWO President Tan Sri Fatimah bte Haji Hashim and Honorary Secretary General F.R. Bhupalan discussed the recommendation with then Minister for Justice Dato' Haji Abdul Rahman Yaacob. In March 1968, the Married Women and Children (Enforcement of Maintenance) Act 1968 was passed. Under this Act, the payment of maintenance to a divorced woman or guardian of a child was ensured by having employers deduct the amounts stated in the court order.

The rights of Muslim women were also on the minds of the women activists of NCWO although they were more cautious in raising issues thought to be contentious (Ng, Mohamad and tan 2006). The Association of Women Lawyers, an affiliate of NCWO, together with the Sisters in Islam, submitted a memorandum on the Reform of the Islamic Family Laws on Polygamy to then Prime Minister Datuk Seri Mahathir bin Mohamad in December 1996 (Abidah 2004). The memorandum recommended the fulfilment of five conditions in addition to consultation with the existing wife before a man is granted the right to take on another wife. The conditions included: counselling for the husband, the existing wife, and wife-to-be; adding a clause to the standard *ta'liq* agreement (the condition stipulated in the marriage certificate, which the husband cites in the presence of a *kadi*, that provides an instance of divorce if the condition is breached), allowing for divorce in cases of desertion, non-maintenance or cruelty; granting the existing wife the right to divorce her husband if he takes on another wife without her consent; increasing the penalty for polygamy without the consent of the courts; and establishing a common registrar of marriages to ascertain if an applicant has been married before.

This was followed by a memorandum, submitted to the government in March 1997, aimed at reforming Islamic family laws. Amendments to the Islamic Family Law (Federal Territory) Act 1984 calls for the Syariah Court to make a final order or orders for the custody and maintenance of dependent children, for the maintenance and accommodation of the divorced wife, and for the payment of *mut'ah* (a portion of a husband's wealth that is transferred to his ex-wife upon divorce provided the divorce was not caused by her) to her (Abidah 2004). The concept of *nusyuz* (disobedience) was also taken up as an issue. While the concept had often been applied to women, the memorandum recommended a provision be added to the Act which makes it an offence for a husband to commit *nusyuz* if he fails to provide his wife with adequate maintenance and other similar entitlements laid out in Islamic law.

Domestic violence was another concern of the Malaysian women activists. In 1989, the NCWO, together with the Joint Action Group against Violence Against Women (JAG-VAW) succeeded in proposing a bill against domestic violence. After three years of reworking it, during which numerous campaigns against domestic violence were staged, the bill was finally submitted to the government (Ng, Mohamad and tan 2006).

Similar non-governmental organizations followed in the footsteps of the NCWO and JAG-VAW. Some groups addressing domestic violence included the Women's Aid Organisation (WAO), All Action Women's Society Malaysia (AWAM), Sisters in Islam (SIS), Women's Crisis Centre (later called Women's Centre for Change), Women's Development Collective (WDC), to name a few (Ng, Mohamad and tan 2006). Many of the organizations, however, were dominated by middle-class tertiary-educated women. Because of this, among other reasons, these women were not able to "spread the notion of women's rights and equality" and thereby impact the larger community of women which tended largely to be fragmented by ethnic identity (Ng, Mohamad and tan 2006, p. 26).

But some organizations, such as the Sisters in Islam, continued to campaign against issues such as polygamy. In 2003, the organization in collaboration with eleven women's organizations under the rubric of "Women's Rights in Islam" in their campaign "called on men to strictly observe a

monogamous marriage and to shun the right to polygyny as
advocated by Islam" (Ng, Mohamad and tan 2006, p. 101).
But their efforts were curtailed by fractures within the
larger Islamic women's activist community. The other
women's Islamic organizations opposed the agenda of
the Sisters in Islam, arguing that polygyny was a male
right and campaigning for monogamy would derail the
integrity and authority of Islam. But the women activists
of that time had one point in their favour: the federal
government adopted a moderate position on Islamic law
to ensure women's contribution to national development
and modernization (Verma 2002). In this regard, the
government had a vested interest in guaranteeing greater
legal protection for women.

National Legislative Protections for Women: "A Glass Half Empty?"

In spite of the numerous pieces of protection legislation in
place for women in Indonesia, Malaysia, and Thailand, gaps
continue to exist in these laws, leaving women partially
rather than fully protected by the law. In relation to
family or matrimonial law, polygamy, divorce, inheritance,
domestic violence, and marital rape continue to be
contentious areas in which gender inequality remains. Not
only do gaps exist in some of these laws, but in the more
comprehensive laws it has also been found that the lack
of enforcement has been a critical factor in perpetuating
women's subordination. For these reasons, women activists
in these countries have found themselves having to monitor
these laws in their quest for gender equality.

A Bone of Contention: Polygamy

Polygamy is one arena in which gender inequality is distinctly played out. Interestingly, addressing polygamy by way of either placing a ban or regulation on it is a common thread in all the national laws on family or marriage in Singapore and Thailand, as well as Indonesia and Malaysia, where Islam's influence is most greatly felt. In Indonesia, the law explicitly grants the individual the right to adhere to the respective regulations laid down in his/ her religion in contracting a marriage (Asian Development Bank 2002). This law has been in force although religious teachings on marriage contradict Indonesian national laws on marriage and divorce. But religion and, in this case, Islam, is not the only variable intersecting with national laws on family or marriage. Customary law in the region continues to be equally strong in influencing how a marriage is contracted.

In Indonesia, it was fairly easy for a Muslim man to take more than one wife before the promulgation of the 1974 Marriage Law. Although the Marriage Law has been interpreted to curb the practice of polygamy and endorse monogamy as the ideal marriage set-up, there have been conflicting assertions put forth that the Marriage Law is essentially ambiguous on this issue (Butt 1999). Some have maintained that the law allows a man to take more than one wife if he is able to seek permission from a religious court. In this case, the protection a woman receives is "more apparent than real" since it would be difficult for her to refuse her husband's wishes (Asian Development Bank 2002, p. 45). But while the right to polygamy has been retained, because bureaucratic procedures to taking on additional wives are so complicated, this has had the effect of "severely limit[ing] the possibility of its arbitrary use" (Butt 1999, p. 127), thereby regulating the practice.[6]

Evidence indicates, however, that religious courts do not always adopt the Marriage Law in polygamy cases. Instead these courts have been found to adhere to Islamic law and allow polygamous marriages to be established. The one push factor for the judges of religious courts being sympathetic to requests for polygamous marriages was the powers of the *mahkamah agung* (Supreme Court). Others cite the inadequate training in secular or civil laws of religious court judges who were trained mainly in interpretations of the *syariah* that favour polygamy. But because of the Religious Court Law of 1989, religious court judges are now civil servants holding academic qualifications. Since this legal move, Islamic judges are more hesitant to contest state laws on the polygamy issue (Butt 1999). The result of the Religious Court Law has had a profound effect: religious court judges now see themselves as part of the state bureaucracy and more of them favour monogamy over polygamy.

In spite of the existence of the Marriage Law, polygamy is not unheard of. That the practice remains is evident in the number of fines imposed on offenders. Moreover, because the fines for polygamy are not hefty, they have not served as deterrents. In particular, men from the rural areas, with lower levels of education, have argued that it is their right under *adat* (custom/tradition) to engage in polygamy. In contrast, men from the middle class, with some exceptions, have generally been found to shun polygamous marriages. But it could be possible that fewer among them have polygamous marriages because they know they have to seek judicial permission, if they wish to take on an additional wife (Butt 1999). The corruption rampant in courts and the procedural hurdles in establishing a polygamous marriage have proven to be sufficient obstacles. This has been the case in Indonesia in spite of evidence from other Islamic countries showing that "economics" or "affordability" is a significant factor for polygamy.

Shifting to the Thai context, gender inequality as encapsulated in the practice of polygamy continues to remain in spite of the Family Law. While the law endorses monogamy, polygamy is taken "lightly as a form of perjury" (Asian Development Bank 2002, p. 47). The inefficiencies of the central marriage registration system are partly to be blamed for the persistence of polygamous marriages. In the past, there was no legal provision criminalizing polygamous marriages nor were women granted the right to divorce their husbands because of polygamy. A woman's prerogative to divorce her husband was only possible if she could prove that her husband was providing maintenance to another woman (Somswasdi 2006). But the tables have since been turned on these two issues. Under the new law, women can now divorce their husbands for adultery. But in spite of this advancement for Thai women, there is another issue with which many have to contend. Social stigma continues to be attached to a divorced woman, thus discouraging many victims from taking the step to file for divorce.

Another Bone of Contention: Divorce

Divorce is another area in which men and women are not on level playing field. In Malaysia and Indonesia, Islamic law governs matrimonial issues and women are disproportionately the aggrieved party in most instances (Endut 2005). For example, the law grants the husband the unilateral right to pronounce a divorce, although the way in which a woman seeks a separation differs across the countries in the region.[7] In this regard, a Muslim woman is disadvantaged in two respects. First, if she wishes to contest her husband's separation from her, her only recourse is to approach the court. But to do so is not necessarily a problem-free process since women do not necessarily have easy access to the courts. For example in Malaysia, where each of the thirteen states and federal territories has independent legislative and judicial jurisdictions over Islamic law, it is not uncommon for a woman to have contracted a marriage in a different state from which she resides. In such a case, if a woman wishes to seek separation, she faces two obstacles: first, she will find it difficult to prove that she falls within the jurisdiction of a particular court if her marriage was contracted in another state; in this case, the enforcement of a judgement becomes near impossible if her husband from whom she is seeking separation resides in another state. Second, it must be noted that a woman does not have the same freedom her husband has should she seek separation; the dissolution of her marriage is only possible if she applies for an order for the separation through the courts.

Husbands have an advantage in another respect: they have been found to pronounce divorce arbitrarily because of the limited sentencing jurisdictions of the courts. In Malaysia, for example, men are not allowed to pronounce divorce on their wives outside the court without the latter's consent (Endut 2005). If they go ahead with insisting on a divorce, fines will have to be incurred. But courts receiving the fines usually declare the pronouncement of divorce to be valid and, in doing so, favour husbands seeking separation from their wives. Moreover, although a divorce can only take place in the court, if a man repudiates his wife outside the court, the divorce is still held to be valid. In this case, the man merely incurs a fine and the divorce is settled. The persistence of such problems may be linked to "an all-male judiciary" that is partial to men seeking a divorce while "exacerbat[ing] Muslim women's disadvantaged access to competent legal representation due to their comparative lack of social, economic, cultural and symbolic capitals" (Maznah 2000, p. 63, as cited in Bong 2006, p. 226). To put it differently, the persistence of patriarchy in the courts is a significant reason for women being disadvantaged in matters of divorce.

The guardianship of children in a divorce also presents problems to women. While major decisions about the child's well-being and property are deemed to be the father's, the physical care of a child is usually left to the mother. Divorced women usually find this arrangement problematic because they are unable to decide on matters such as the children's birth registration and schooling (Endut 2005).

Up until 1999, non-Muslim women in Malaysia also faced discrimination. Only men were granted parental

authority and were the sole legal guardians of a child
and his/her property (OECD n.d.).[8] Although the Law
Reform Act provided for the custody and maintenance of
children, the Guardianship of Infants Act (1961) did not
grant women equal rights (Asian Development Bank 2002).
It was a Cabinet directive in 1999 that turned the tables,
giving women, regardless of religious affiliation, as much
parental authority as men. In cases of divorce, both men
and women are granted the same right to custody. This
move was in stark contrast to the laws governing custody
earlier on where the father was automatically considered the
guardian of a child. If he was deceased, the mother might
be granted this right, although the court had the capacity to
appoint another male guardian if it saw fit. But if the father
was still living and could not be found, or was considered
unfit to look after the child, or abusive, the mother had to
appeal for the guardianship of the child, which might not
have been automatically granted. Moreover, women found
in this situation usually faced a host of other problems,
such as trying to obtain official documents for the child,
and hiring legal representation.

In Thailand, some measure of gender equality has been
attained in divorce. In the past, both men and women had
the right to divorce on judicial grounds, but in the case of
adultery, women were discriminated by the law since only
men were allowed to divorce their wives on this ground. A
woman could not divorce her husband because of a single
act of adultery on his part unless she is able to prove that
her husband maintains and honours another woman as his
mia noi (minor wife) and, in effect, is committing bigamy
(Asian Development Bank 2002). This was the law based

on a Cabinet decision in April 1996. In 2007, the National Legislative Assembly revised the law so that women have the same right as men to divorce their spouses on the ground of adultery.[9] However the bar has been raised; only repeated acts of adultery are justification for divorce for both men and women alike. In spite of this advancement for women, they continue to be disadvantaged in a related matter. In the case of divorce, it is common for children to be left in the custody of women. But many a times, because of the inefficiencies of the judicial system, divorced woman are left without alimony or child support from their former husbands.

The laws on divorce, however, can be relatively harsh on male civil servants. In a divorce, the court has the right to insist that a levy on the income of the husband/father is set aside as maintenance payment for the child (Asian Development Bank 2002). Although divorced women may benefit from this law, its reach is only limited to wives seeking separation from male civil servants. The other complication is that many divorces and separations do not necessarily go through the legal system, thus leaving the divorced or separated woman with little legal and economic protection.

"And Yet Another": The Inheritance Issue

According to Islam, daughters inherit a smaller share of the ancestral property compared with sons, and a widower is entitled to a larger share than a widow. In Indonesia, the Civil Code, however, does not discriminate against either sex in the case of inheritance. But family law tempered by local cultural practices may prove to be disadvantageous to women (Asian Development Bank 2002). The patrilineal system, which favours the agnatic son (usually the firstborn), practised among the Batak of North Sumatra, the Lampung of Sumatra, the Balinese, and the Roti Islanders of Eastern Nusa Tenggara, is an example. But in most parts of the archipelago, the parental system, in which both sons and daughters have equal rights to inheritance of an estate, tends to be the model. Here, both husband and wife are not only equal partners in a marriage, but also have equal rights to property based on the law (Lukito 2005).

In Malaysia, Muslim women face discrimination in so far as inheritance rules are concerned because they are predominantly adherents of the Shafii school of law. The Shafii system of inheritance under *faraid* stipulates that daughters may receive half the share due to sons while male agnatic relatives are also given prominence as residuary heirs.[10] In the absence of a male agnatic heir, the Baitulmal[11] may claim the residuary share. Women have the right to inherit half of what a man is entitled to inherit, presumably because he is responsible for the maintenance of the children (Asian Development Bank 2002).

Civil laws governing inheritance were equally gender-biased at one time. According to the Distribution Act of 1958, a woman whose husband did not leave a will was entitled to only one third of the property if they had children, and one half if they were childless (OECD n.d.).[12] But if a woman died without leaving a will, her property was automatically transferred to the husband, regardless of whether they had children. Since 1997, inheritance laws have been amended to become gender-neutral.

Women members of the NCWO should be credited for their unabated effort in fighting for amendments to the provisions under the Distribution Act 1958. As far back as 1967 in a paper on "The Status of Women in Malaysia in regard to Law, Marriage and Family Life", then Honorary Secretary Mrs Bhupalan argued that:

> ... there seems to be no conceivable reason why half of a man's assets ... should go to his parents and in the event of their demise to rather distant relatives. Why should the wife not be amply provided for in her old age? Why should the wife not enjoy the fruits of their joint labour? Yet, on the other hand, despite the fact that there may be children, or a wife may have inherited her assets from her family, her husband obtains complete control of her estate if she dies intestate. This is unjust and does not, apart from the gross injustice to women, protect the children ... (Abidah 2004, p. 142).

Thailand's matrimonial laws on property rights are also problematic. The Family Law is biased because it endorses the transfer of property from a woman to a man on their marriage. This discriminates against women especially since the property she brings into a marriage is intended to be a source of economic security for her in the case of a divorce (Mertus 1995). Women are belittled in another way: the law allows the parents, guardian, or adopter of a woman to accept property from a man in return for her agreeing to the marriage (Somswasdi 2006). What this practice does is to commodify the woman as she becomes an object to be exchanged between the families.

"The Final Straw": The Plagues of Domestic Violence and Marital Rape

Domestic violence and marital rape call to question the notion of the home as a haven. Studies have found that women are more vulnerable to becoming physically attacked, injured, or killed in her own home by someone to whom she is related either biologically or by marriage than in any other social context (Macionis and Plummer 2002). While anatomical differences explain why women are often the victims and men the aggressors, beyond anatomy, domestic violence is linked to how masculinity and femininity are socially constructed: men are socialized from young into learning that it is acceptable for them to demonstrate their masculinity through physical force, even on women, while women are taught to accept aggressive male behaviour. Furthermore, patriarchal ideology promotes the idea that men are masters to be obeyed and that women should play a subservient role (cf. Dobash and Dobash 1980).

In Southeast Asia, as in much of other parts of Asia, there are strong socio-cultural expectations of the "good, docile and obedient woman". Within this context, it is the assumed power in the hands of the man that leads him to justify his actions against a woman. For example, in Thailand the normative view of women is that they are expected to be wives and mothers and that they will fulfil their spiritual obligations through their domestic duties. The "ideal image of a woman [is that she is] a devoted, faithful, and obedient wife and mother ..." (Peach 2006, p. 33). Hence, should domestic violence erupt in the family, it is considered a private affair to be sorted out by the respective parties (Somswasdi 2006). But that prevailing gendered image has been contested especially by educated Thai women, as evidenced in the issue of domestic violence. Women activists in Thailand have been lobbying actively for an anti-domestic violence bill. Although legal protections were written into the 1997 Constitution, providing some level of protection to victims of domestic violence, gender inequality on this issue continued to prevail. The 2003 case of a university lecturer who beat his wife to death with a golf club and umbrella, spurring a series of strident campaigns on the issue, is a case in point (Somswasdi 2005). Women's groups became highly critical of the court's decision because the reduced punishment for the offender clearly demonstrated the male bias of the court. Because the prosecutor did not plan to submit an appeal, women's groups staged protests, putting pressure on the prosecutor to reverse the sentence. Since then, the case has made it to the Supreme Court. Although the outcome was disappointing, the case fuelled women's groups to fight for an anti-domestic violence bill.

Their efforts did not go to waste as the Domestic Violence Victim Protection Act was passed in November 2007. Under this law, victims and witnesses of domestic violence have the legal right to take their cases up to the police and thereafter to a prosecutor. Convicted abusers may face jail sentences of up to six months and/or a fine.

Marital rape has also been an issue heavily contested by women activists. After being written into the national agenda in 2003, marital rape is now criminalized in Thailand (Peach 2006). In June 2007, the National Legislative

Assembly of Thailand passed a law criminalizing marital rape. Under this law, the definition of rape has been broadened to include all forms of forced sex. If convicted of rape, offenders could receive sentences of up to twenty years in prison and a fine.[13] Prior to this, marital rape found endorsement in Section 1461 of the Family Law, which underscores the point that a husband can demand sexual intercourse from his wife whenever he desires, even against her wishes. The Penal Code of 1956 did not cover marital rape either; rape was instead referred to as a sexual offence against a woman who is not the wife of a man (Somswasdi 2006).

Unlike Thailand, Malaysian law only recognizes the act of violence in marital rape and not the rape itself as a criminal offence, owing to the amendment in the Penal Code which took effect in September 2007. The penalties for marital violence when a husband beats his wife to have sex with her are up to twenty years' imprisonment and whipping. While this is a step forward, there has been some skepticism since the burden of proof continues to rest on the victim with her word against her husband's. Furthermore, the Women's Aid Organisation, which renders help to victims of domestic violence and their children, maintains that "marital rape", as it is covered in the recent amendment in the Penal Code, is limited since it does not include instances in which the husband uses threats against his wife to make her submit to him such as threatening to divorce her, to take the children away from her, or to go to a sex worker instead if she refuses him sex.

Other forms of domestic violence in a marriage are also a crime in Malaysia under the Domestic Violence

Act. Passed in 1994, it took women activists eleven years to see the Act enacted (Josiah 2003). Before the Act was passed, the police were not obliged to help a victim partly because domestic violence was seen as a private problem to be sorted out by the husband and wife themselves, rather than an issue requiring the intervention of public institutions represented by the police, courts, and welfare agencies. In doing so, the police, in turn, "normalise[d]" such behaviour, shifting the blame from the husband to the couple instead (Abbott, Wallace and Tyler 2005, p. 295). Besides, there continues to be a strong cultural value placed on men as disciplinarians of women's errant behaviour (Chan 2001). In this light, it is not surprising that many policemen have been found to advise the victim to return to the perpetrator of the violence (Ng, Mohamad and tan 2006).

Although women's groups view the implementation of the Domestic Violence Act as a "monumental achievement ... to the seriousness with which [the] community regards domestic violence", it has been acknowledged that the existing Act has its drawbacks and, therefore, there is a need to strengthen it to provide greater protection to victims (Josiah 2003, n.p.). For example, it has been pointed out that the term "violence" is too narrowly defined as it only covers physical violence while discounting psychological and emotional harm (Amirthalingam 2005). Furthermore, the Act must be interpreted together with the Penal Code and the Criminal Procedure Code. While on the positive side, this has allowed for the Domestic Violence Act to become part of the criminal legislation so that it can be applied to all Malaysian women whether Muslim or non-Muslim (Ng, Mohamad and tan 2006),[14] however, as the Act has to be read with the Penal Code and the Criminal

Procedure Code, this has created "confusion and inconsistent application, resulting in weak judgments and inadequate enforcement of penalties ..." (Asian Development Bank 2002, p. 83).

Another problem is that because the Act has to be read together with the Penal Code and the Criminal Procedure Code, most of the offences fall under the "non-seizable" category. What this means is that an investigation order is required from the deputy public prosecutor before the police will investigate the complaint. But this lengthy process compromises the victim's access to immediate protection. The Domestic Violence Act disadvantages women in another way. While allowing for the "exclusion of the abuser from the shared home by granting the right of exclusive possession to the victim", courts, however, have the right to revoke this order if alternative shelter is available to the victim (Amirthalingam 2005, p. 691). What this implies is that the abused woman ends up having to depend on relatives and friends and, in turn, "los[ing] the comfort and security of the home ... [a situation which creates] a devastating form of disempowerment [for the victim]" (Amirthalingam 2005, p. 691).

The Women's Aid Organisation has also found problems with the law. Documented cases of women being forced to approach three different places to report complaints and waiting for extended periods of time for the appropriate assistance, both of which involve costs and time off from work, are rife.[15] In addition, some welfare officers have been often found to block women from filing reports against their abusers by either delaying the process or convincing them to return to their husbands or abusers. Moreover, waiting time for Personal Protection Orders (PPOs) ranging from two days to more than four months becomes detrimental to the victim's safety, especially if she is waiting for a court hearing on her case.[16] Besides, the terms on the actual compensation for personal injuries, damage to property, or financial loss remain unclear, and how the compensation is to be determined and obtained from the perpetrator is equally ambiguous (Asian Development Bank 2002).

Indonesia has seen a major breakthrough in its legal system for addressing domestic violence. Before the anti-domestic violence legislation came in force in September 2004, the term "domestic violence" was not even spelled out in the Criminal Code; instead the phrase "an act of maltreatment" was used (Asian Development Bank 2002, p. 82). In addition, punishments were also fairly lenient. The Law of Republic of Indonesia No. 23/2004 regarding the Elimination of Violence in Household was a result of decades of effort on the part of women's rights advocates' activities. Four forms of violence are criminalized under the present law: physical, psychological, sexual (including marital rape), and economic neglect. Under the law, the police, prosecutors, and other actors linked to the judicial system have defined roles to play in addressing a domestic violence case.[17] In addition, the law now implicitly suggests that these actors cannot brush aside a domestic violence case, treating it as a private matter to be left in the hands of family members to resolve. Before the law was in place, the criminal code demanded two witnesses for a conviction to be ascertained. Under the new law, it only takes one person — namely the victim or a witness — to bring the case forward to the authorities.

Implementation of the law, however, has met with obstacles. Many courts have been found to insist on two witnesses instead of one. Punishments have also been relatively light, just like it was in the past before the law came into effect. Thus, women's groups have found themselves deep in fighting for another cause — ensuring that the law is implemented effectively and information on the law is disseminated across the country.

"The Women's Charter": How Protected Are Singapore Women?

The fight for women's rights is not unique to any one particular country in the region. Evidence from three countries in Southeast Asia — Indonesia, Malaysia, and Thailand — reveal striking parallels in terms of how women collectively have played an instrumental role in the development and enforcement of laws protecting their rights. As in the other Southeast Asian countries such as Indonesia, Malaysia and Thailand, it was the educated women in Singapore who were at the forefront of fighting patriarchy and confronting gender inequality; it was this group of women who had been exposed to feminist ideas and saw the necessity to change the course of their destiny. The most pressing issues that concerned these women were polygamy, divorce, inheritance issues, and domestic violence.

Independence in these countries was a turning point for many women concerned about their rights. In the years before independence, politicized women were more accepting of the male argument that attention to "female concerns" should be secondary until after independence was attained. But once independence was achieved, an increasing number of governments explicitly demonstrated their commitment to gender equality, as it was in the case of Singapore.

The Women's Charter Ordinance No. 18 of 1961 represented a complete breakthrough in Singapore's history of family law. Up until 1961, legislation had provided for only Muslim and Christian marriages and, for them, secular registry marriage was an option. The Chinese and Hindus had been left to celebrate marriages, whether of first or secondary wives, in whatever customary style they chose, with the absence of regularization by official registration. As Ann Wee demonstrates in Chapter 2, because no fixed customary requirements were ever identified, this system led to a never-ending history of contentious litigation in respect of intestate estates over the question of who was or was not legally married by customary standards. Although from time to time the colonial government dabbled with measures to regulate customary marriage, they met with a huge range of conflicting opinions, mainly from the Chinese community.

By the 1950s, English-educated women in Singapore were becoming active in movements seeking change, especially for legal reform that would establish all (non-Muslim) marriages to be monogamous. However, there was no radical activism on their part, although they had become increasingly conscious of the injustices of patriarchy and gender inequality. It was this group of women — exposed as they were to feminist ideas — which saw the necessity to change the course of their

destiny; but unaccustomed to radical action, they made
rather modest beginnings in converting consciousness
into struggle. In striking contrast were the Chinese-
educated young women. For them, the most pressing
issues were polygamy, divorce, and the exploitation of
women in prostitution. With these women putting their
political shoulders to the PAP general election wheel,
the Women's Charter in its final form was an inevitable
outcome, Ann Wee argues.

What then in substantial terms is the Women's Charter
and how does it protect Singapore women? The Charter
must be treated to be in essence a family law prescribing
the obligations of both husband and wife as good partners
and parents. In other words, by reinscribing that marriage
should be perceived as "the equal cooperative partnership
of different kinds of efforts for the mutual well-being
of the spouses", the legislation aims to place women
and men on equal footing with each other. In economic
matters, the courts are entrusted with the right to enforce
orders that are fair and equitable in a troubled marriage.
In Chapter 3, Leong Wai Kum, however, cautions that
the Charter is far from being a perfect legislation. In this
regard she says: "Not every aspect of the family law in
Singapore is above criticism and there are indeed areas
where improvements can easily be made but it is, by and
large, a set of laws that we can all be proud of."

But because the Charter does not protect the rights
of married women to the exclusion of men, it is widely
acknowledged that the term "Women's Charter" is a
misnomer. Although its objectives are to regulate — among
other things — marriage, the rights and obligations of

married couples towards each other and in relation to their child/children, and to provide for the rights and liabilities of couples when they divorce, divorcing couples — who do not receive what they would like, or who demand more than what the court has adjudicated to be just and equitable — often view the Charter as an unfair, unjust, and lopsided piece of legislation. In Chapter 4, Ellen Lee points out the shortcomings of the Charter by highlighting the areas of contention related to issues of divorce, namely, custody, care and control, and access to the child/children, maintenance for them, financial support for the wife seeking the separation, division of matrimonial assets, the matrimonial home, and costs of proceedings. In addition, disputes also arise in other areas such as the enforcement of court orders, whether in respect of maintenance, protection orders, access, or realization of the entitlement after division of the matrimonial assets.

As in the national laws protecting women's rights of other countries in Southeast Asia, the Singapore Women's Charter has undergone revisions in the time of its existence. While the revision to the Women's Charter in 1996 widened the definition of family violence and facilitated greater enforcement to accord more safety and provision of support strategies to victims, women, and children affected, it also brought to the fore other groups of vulnerable persons who fall through the safety net of the legal provisions. Sudha Nair in Chapter 5 demonstrates how the law sometimes impacts on families experiencing violence in ways it may not have foreseen. Because family violence is a very complex issue, the situation is exacerbated for vulnerable members of the family when compounded by divorce and ancillary matters related to child custody/access and maintenance. In uncovering the issues relating to divorce in cases of family violence, gaps in the current system are revealed and suggestions to facilitate greater empowerment cum support to vulnerable persons in intimate relationships are raised.

Notes

1. The term domestic violence refers to family violence. While the term domestic violence is used throughout the first chapter, in the rest of the chapters of the book, the term family violence is used instead by the respective authors in keeping with Section 64 of the Women's Charter.
2. See Murtaza Mandli-Yadav, "RIGHTS: CEDAW'S Mixed Findings on Progress for Women", Inter Press Service, 13 July 1998 <http://web.archive.org/web/20040214095325/http://www.oneworld.org/ips2/jul98/16_02_060.html> (accessed 14 May 2009).
3. See UNIFEM, n.d., "Say No to Violence against Women" <http://www.unifem.org/campaigns/vaw/issue.php> (accessed 14 May 2009).
4. See "20th Anniversary of Women's Convention: Time to Take Women's Human Rights Seriously" <http://www.amnesty.org/en/library/asset/IOR51/006/1999/en/50026f2c-225a-4d7f-b31f-040d1e961bef/ior510061999en.pdf> (accessed 15 May 2009).
5. It must be noted that there are some states that overtly refrain from interfering in the application of religious or customary laws on the basis of respecting culture and tradition, despite having a secular ideology to which the state adheres (Mertus 1995).

6. By way of comparison, it is interesting to note that many states, in which polygamy is endorsed by religious custom, see regulating the practice as the solution rather than an outright ban. Bangladesh is a case in point, although it has been documented that few men follow the law, thereby rendering the law ineffective (Mertus 1995).

7. Although Muslim men have the unilateral right to divorce their wives, women are not completely denied this right although they might face problems in carrying this through. In the state of Kelantan in Malaysia, as in many other states in the country, it was found that if a wife applies for a *ta'liq* divorce to which her husband refuses, she is usually persuaded by the *kadi* (a judge in Muslim affairs who handles Muslim marriage applications and solemnizes marriages) and the *hakam* (arbitrator) to accept a *khulo* divorce (a divorce requested by the wife and is granted by the husband upon the wife paying him a sum of money or an amount in kind) (Siraj 1994). In this case, she ends up having to "bribe" her husband into accepting a *talaq* divorce (a "release" divorce) by paying him a sum. Although the sums are not great, poorer women seeking a divorce see this payment as a financial burden.

8. See OECD, n.d., Social Institutions and Gender Index, "Gender Equality and Social Institutions in Malaysia" <http://genderindex.org/country/malaysia> (accessed 18 November 2009).

9. See "Feminism and Thailand Law", *Thailand Law Blog*, 2 December 2008, <http://thailawforum.com/blog/feminism-and-thailand-law> (accessed 22 July 2010).

10. The Shafii approach to inheritance is essentially the pre-Islamic Arabian customary law. Patriarchal in character, it must be highlighted that the Shafii approach stands in

contradistinction to Malay customary laws which grants either equal shares toward males and females or even, under the matrilineal *adat perpatih* system, enables females to be the holders of family property. But customary laws are now labelled as "un-Islamic" and condemned, even though some scholars have suggested that there are "devices" within the Islamic framework to accommodate such laws that provide fairer shares towards women in the form of trusts, endowments, and testamentary bequests.

11. The Baitulmal is the institution that acts as a trustee for Muslims, looking after assets which are beneficial to members of the Muslim community.

12. See OECD, n.d., Social Institutions and Gender Index, "Gender Equality and Social Institutions in Malaysia", <http://genderindex.org/country/malaysia> (accessed 18 November 2009).

13. In spite of the rape law (Article 276) in the Penal Code already in place, conservative state agencies have been fighting hard to bring back the old law, arguing that the current rape law makes it difficult to prosecute the perpetrators because its definition is too broad. The draft amendment drawn up by conservative elements in government have also argued that imprisonment is not justifiable because marital rape is a private affair. On the definition of rape in the current law, some legal practitioners have maintained that it would be more effective to differentiate offences and to have the law deal with each separately. As of the time of writing this chapter, police officers, social workers, and academics have been discussing the practical implications of the law, and adjustments to the law are yet to be made. See "Altering Rape Law is Wrong", *Bangkok Post Opinion*, 30 October 2009 <http://www.bangkokpost.com/opinion/26532/altering-rape-law-is-wrong> (accessed 30 June 2010).

14. Irrespective of how the law may be interpreted, it has been asserted that this piece of legislation epitomizes the closing of the "battle over (secular versus religious) turf" fought by women NGOs in their ten-year lobby for a law to address domestic violence (Bong 2006, p. 227). This is because it is the only law that applies to both Muslim and non-Muslim women.
15. See "Shining a Bright Light: Monitoring a Domestic Violence Law in Malaysia" <http://www.unifem.org/gender_issues/voices_from_the_field/story.php?StoryID=329> (accessed 19 May 2009).
16. See "Domestic Violence" <http://www.wao.org.my/research/domesticviolence.htm> (accessed 19 May 2009).
17. See Ratna Bataramunti, "Justice for Women? New Anti-Domestic Violence Law Brings Hope for Women", 2006, <http://www.insideindonesia.org/content/view/64/29/> (accessed 21 May 2009).

References

Abbott, Pamela, Claire Wallace, and Melissa Tyler. *An Introduction to Sociology: Feminist Perspectives*. London: Routledge, 2005.

Abidah Amin. "Women's Rights Relating to Marriage". In *Empowering Women in Malaysia: The Mission Continues ...* [History of the National Council of Women's Organisations, Malaysia: 1960–2000]. Petaling Jaya, Selangor: The National Council of Women's Organisations, Malaysia, 2004.

"Altering Rape Law is Wrong". *Bangkok Post Opinion*, 30 October 2009. <http://www.bangkokpost.com/opinion/26532/altering-rape-law-is-wrong> (accessed 30 June 2010).

Amirthalingam, K. "Women's Rights, International Norms, and Domestic Violence: Asian Perspectives". *Human Rights Quarterly* 27 (2005): 683–708.

"20th Anniversary of Women's Convention: Time to Take Women's Human Rights Seriously". <http://www.amnesty.org/en/library/asset/IOR51/006/1999/en/50026f2c-225a-4d7f-b31f-040d1e961bef/ior510061999en.pdf> (accessed 15 May 2009).

Asian Development Bank. *Sociolegal Status of Women in Indonesia, Malaysia, Philippines, and Thailand.* Manila: Asian Development Bank, 2002.

Bataramunti, Ratna. "Justice for Women? New Anti-Domestic Violence Law Brings Hope for Women", 2006. <http://www.insideindonesia.org/content/view/64/29/> (accessed 21 May 2009).

Bong, Sharon A. *The Tension Between Women's Rights and Religions: The Case of Malaysia.* New York: The Edwin Mellen Press, 2006.

Butt, Simon. "Polygamy and Mixed Marriage in Indonesia: The Application of the Marriage Law in the Courts". In *Indonesia: Law and Society*, edited by T. Lindsey. Sydney: The Federation Press, 1999.

Chan, C. "Malaysia Old and New: A Visitor's Perspective". *Harvard Asia Pacific Review* 5, no. 1 (2001): 69–70.

Chandrakirana, Kamala and Yuniyanti Chuzaifah. "The Battle over a 'New' Indonesia: Religious Extremism, Democratization and Women's Agency in a Plural Society". In *Muslim Women and the Challenge of Islamic Extremism*, edited by N. Othman. Petaling Jaya: Sisters in Islam, 2005.

Dobash, R. Emerson and Russell Dobash. *Violence against Wives: A Case against the Patriarchy.* Shepton Mallet: Open Books, 1980.

"Domestic Violence". <http://www.wao.org.my/research/domesticviolence.htm> (accessed 19 May 2009).

Economic and Social Commission for Asia and the Pacific. *Human Rights and Legal Status of Women in the Asian and Pacific Region.* New York: United Nations, 1997.

Endut, Noraida. "Overview of the Legal Systems in Southeast Asia". In *Encyclopedia of Women and Islamic Cultures* 2, edited by S. Joseph et al. Netherlands: Brill, 2005.

"Feminism and Thailand Law". *Thailand Law Blog*, 2 December 2008. <http://thailawforum.com/blog/feminism-and-thailand-law> (accessed 22 July 2010).

Josiah, Ivy. "Malaysian Women's Campaign for the Domestic Violence Act". Paper presented at the Roundtable Discussion, "Strengthening Policy Participation Partnerships between Government and Civil Society". National Council of Women's Organisations, 19 August 2003.

Lukito, Ranto. "The Main Features of *Adat* Inheritance Law". In *Encyclopedia of Women and Islamic Cultures* 2, edited by S. Joseph et al. Netherlands: Brill, 2005.

Macionis, John and Ken Plummer. *Sociology: A Global Introduction*. 2nd ed. London: Prentice Hall, 2002.

Mandli-Yadav, Murtaza. "RIGHTS: CEDAW'S Mixed Findings on Progress for Women", 1998. <http://web.archive.org/web/20040214095325/http://www.oneworld.org/ips2/jul98/16_02_060.html> (accessed 14 May 2009).

Mertus, Julie. "State Discriminatory Family Law and Customary Abuses". In *Women's Rights, Human Rights: International Feminist Perspectives*, edited by J. Peters and A. Wolper. New York: Routledge, 1995.

Mezey, Susan G. "Law and Equality: The Continuing Struggle for Women's Rights". In *Issues in Feminism: An Introduction to Women's Studies*, 5th ed., edited by S. Ruth. Mountain View, California: Mayfield Publishing, 2001.

Ng, Cecilia, Mohamad Maznah, and tan beng hui. *Feminism and the Women's Movement in Malaysia: An Unsung (R)evolution*. London: Routledge, 2006.

OECD, n.d. Social Institutions and Gender Index. "Gender Equality and Social Institutions in Malaysia". <http://genderindex.org/country/malaysia> (accessed 18 November 2009).

Peach, Lucinda. "Sex or Sangha? Non-normative Gender Roles for Women in Thai Law and Religion". In *Mixed Blessings: Laws, Religions, and Women's Rights in the Asia-Pacific Region*, edited by A. Whiting and C. Evans. Leidin: Martinus Nijhoff Publishers, 2006.

Robinson, Kathryn. "Muslim Women's Political Struggle for Marriage Law Reform in Contemporary Indonesia". In *Mixed Blessings: Laws, Religions, and Women's Rights in the Asia-Pacific Region*, edited by A. Whiting and C. Evans. Leidin: Martinus Nijhoff Publishers, 2006.

"Shining a Bright Light: Monitoring a Domestic Violence Law in Malaysia". <http://www.unifem.org/gender_issues/voices_from_the_field/story.php?StoryID=329> (accessed 19 May 2009).

Siraj, M. "Women and the Law: Significant Developments in Malaysia". *Law and Society Review* 28, no. 3 (1994): 561–72.

Somswasdi, Virada. *With Hindsight, Heading Forward: Integrative Thai Feminist Standpoint*. Chiangmai: Wanida Press, 2006.

———. "The Power of Law and Women's Presence in the Thaksin Era". Paper presented at the Cornell Law School Berger International Speaker Series, Paper no. 5, 2005.

Stivens, Maila. "(Re)framing Women's Rights Claims in Malaysia". In *Malaysia: Islam, Society and Politics*, edited by V. Hooker and N. Othman. Singapore: Institute of Southeast Asian Studies, 2003.

UNIFEM, n.d. "Say No to Violence against Women". <http://www.unifem.org/campaigns/vaw/issue.php> (accessed 14 May 2009).

Verma, V. "Debating Rights in Malaysia: Contradictions and Challenges". *Journal of Contemporary Asia* 32, no. 1 (2002): 108–30.

Wieringa, S.E. "Islamization in Indonesia: Women Activists' Discourses". *Signs: Journal of Women in Culture and Society* 32, no. 1 (2006): 1–8.

2
The Women's Charter, 1961: Where We Were Coming From and How We Got There

Ann Wee

In "The Tasks Ahead" — their manifesto for the June 1959 Singapore General Election — the People's Action Party (PAP) had promised to legislate monogamous marriage and to make other radical improvements to the status of women.[1] By April 1960, the Women's Charter Bill (No. 81 of 1960) was presented to the Legislative Assembly for debate. The bill covered not only family law, but also the protection of young women from exploitation as prostitutes.

The Bill was presented to the Legislative Assembly in truly stirring words:

> We promised this legislation to the electorate and we were moved to do so by deep and profound conviction as to how a good society should be regulated.
>
> — Dr Goh Keng Swee
> (*Singapore Legislative Assembly Debates* [SLAD] 12
> 1960, p. 480)

> This Women's Charter before the House to-day will find a place as a permanent monument and milestone

in the history of the social struggle for the betterment of the world.

> — Dr Lee Siew Choh
> (*Singapore Legislative Assembly Debates* [SLAD] 12
> 1960, p. 454)

In our inhuman, semi-colonial, semi-feudalistic society, the tragedies of women were very common. Women in our society have been like pieces of meat, put on the table for men to slice ... We will liberate women from the hands of the oppressors.

> — Madam Chan Choy Siong (speaking in Mandarin)
> (*Singapore Legislative Assembly Debates* [SLAD] 12
> 1960, p. 443)

We have thought it important that we consider this as something outside the ordinary stream of legislation, we consider it to be in the real sense of the word a Charter for the women of our State.

> — Minister K.M. Byrne
> (*Singapore Legislative Assembly Debates* [SLAD] 12
> 1960, p. 480)

Before the Charter

With good cause the Minister for Labour and Law, K.M. Byrne, in presenting the bill, had described prior legislation relating to women and children as "spread so widely throughout our legislation that it requires the training and experience of a lawyer, to find one's way through" (SLAD 12, 1960, p. 481). This legislation had included, among other pieces of law, the Muslims Ordinance No. 25 of 1957 ("descended" from the Mohammedan Marriage Ordinance No. 5 of 1880) and the Christian Marriage Ordinance No. 10 of 1940 ("descended" from the Christian Marriage Ordinance No. 3 of 1898), and also a much more recent innovation, the Civil Marriage Ordinance No. 9 of 1940, along the lines of the law in Britain.

Apart from these measures and up until that time, the bulk of Chinese and Hindu marriages had been founded on customary celebrations, with no provision whatsoever for statutory registration. Variations, definitions, arguments, and legal decisions galore persisted, and thereby hangs a very long tale indeed.

Sir Benson Maxwell (Chief Justice of the Straits Settlements 1867–71) stated that "in our law polygamy is not only foreign but also repugnant" (Song 1923, p. 121). Nonetheless, he made the "bold and vigorous decision" to give legal recognition to Chinese polygamy" (Braddell 1921, p. 156). Polygamy (or more precisely "polygyny") continued to be legally recognized until the date of the Women's Charter.

Following this decision, the colonial authorities abstained from imposing any statutory regulation on customary marriages of the non-Christian, non-Muslim residents in Singapore. For whom did this abstention have most significance? South Asians who were Muslim or Christian were covered by existing laws. Indians had generally been seen to keep matters of marriage and family back in their land of origin, although there were exceptions.[2]

The Report on the Census of Population 1957 (Singapore) records more than 418,000 married Chinese as against fewer than 59,000 married "Indians and Pakistanis".[3] This latter figure can be assumed to include a sizeable proportion of Muslims, and an unknown number of Christians since data on religion were not collected then. Chinese Christian and (later) registry marriages were a minority (Freedman 1952, p. 105). The census figures tended, therefore, to confirm the impression that up to the time of the Women's Charter, concerns relating to customary marriage had always applied disproportionately to the Chinese community.

Though seeking to abstain from interference, the colonial authorities were forced to rule on what constituted a valid customary marriage. This arose from actions brought to court, contesting rights of inheritance, primarily in the intestate estates of wealthy Chinese. The High Court was forced to decide who had been legally married to the deceased and, therefore, who was entitled to a widow's or legitimate child's share of the estate.

In a case that went up to the Privy Council in London for appeal in 1920, an eminent judge commented that in the West, a child is legitimate because of the validity of the union of the parents, while the converse is true in the case of the Chinese, where custom legitimized the child. This forced the court to decide "that the union from which they come must be regarded as lawful" (Braddell 1921, p. 165). In all instances, the courts were unable to understand that a Chinese child's legitimacy stems from recognition by the father only, the status of the parents' union being irrelevant.

Straits Settlement case reports indicate that the High Court's task in coming to a decision on what constituted a recognized customary marriage was not easy. Numerous experts and Chinese consuls were called in as witnesses, but there were no specific rituals they could agree on that could define a Chinese customary marriage. Marriage customs in China had differed not only between provinces and dialect groups, but there was also evidence of differences even between neighbourhoods within the same province. As such, "Chinese family law is not purely a matter of law, but includes a large number of general usages" (Braddell 1921, p. 165). Moreover, Chinese residents in Singapore and the other Straits Settlements had introduced new components, not known in their ancestral homeland. For these reasons, "the difficulties which our Courts have had to overcome cannot be understated" [*sic*] (Braddell 1921, p. 165).

In seeking to be just to all, the courts applied the British law of intestacy, and gave inheritance rights to all proven wives, and to daughters equally with sons — thus completely contravening Chinese custom which would have entitled all these women to maintenance only, plus marriage expenses for daughters. In this and in the failure to recognize both the nature of legitimacy and of the customary adoption of a son in Chinese families, the colonial courts failed miserably in their intention — as stated in 1807 by Sir Edmund Stanley, first recorder, Penang — of guaranteeing "scrupulous attention to ancient usages and habits" (cited in Purcell 1968, pp. 49–50). To this end, "our law is therefore very clearly neither English nor Chinese law, but a mixture of the two" (Braddell 1921, p. 157).

The Civil Code of the post-1911 Republic of China, which came into force in 1931, included legislation to

regulate marriage. Evidence suggests that this legislation
served mainly as a blueprint for the urban elite, and that it
never had any general application even within China, let
alone among the overseas Chinese. There had also been
a "Reformed", post-1919 "May 4th movement" marriage
system by notification in a newspaper (Freedman 1952,
p. 107).[4] Were the marriages of this style also truly legal?
The issue was never settled.

New-style "full-blown" customary marriages in
Singapore and the Straits Settlements changed from being
a household event to one in the clan hall or other public
meeting place. In Melaka, this included the Chinese Lawn
Tennis Club (Chinese Marriage Committee [CMC] 1926,
p. 120). Ceremonials involved both family members and
such persons as clan association officials and elders. Very
elaborate and beautifully decorated marriage certificates
could be purchased at bookstores, and were signed by the
couple, their guardians, and the clan officials — and a copy
was given to the bride and groom for safe keeping.

I recall vividly numerous varieties of these certificates
being produced in the course of marital disputes when I was
dealing with such matters at the Singapore Department of
Social Welfare. Usually the wife's copy was emblazoned
with a large red and gold phoenix while the husband's with an
equally resplendent dragon. Although not legal documents,
these were treasured as such. The husband who in a fit of
rage destroyed the certificates and/or wedding photographs
caused matrimonial panic, sending his distraught wife
rushing to the Welfare Department, convinced that he had
endangered the legal status of the marriage — which, of
course, was not so.

Clan hall celebrations, elaborate certificates, and studio photography implied families of at least modest means. For the poor, and also for women widowed or of tarnished reputation, there was the "followed marriage", where a couple had set up home together with no ceremony whatsoever (Freedman 1957, p. 173; Wee 1996, p. 15). This was well recognized among Singaporeans as a valid marriage, although of a somewhat less-than-ideal variety. I recall that speakers would lower their voices when recounting that so-and-so's marriage was of this kind.

The eventual ruling was that ceremonials were irrelevant for a legal decision. All that was required to legitimize a customary marriage was "cohabitation and repute" (CMC 1926, p. 152, Sir Roland Braddell's evidence).

The Chinese Marriage Committee (CMC), 1926

The Chinese Marriage Committee (CMC) was established by the government of the Straits Settlements (Singapore, Penang and Malacca) to enquire into the forms of customary marriages and "if thought desirable" (CMC 1926, p. 1) to make recommendations on legislation for both the registration and dissolution of "marriages contracted by Chinese rites and ceremonies" (CMC 1926, p. 1). The committee received both oral and written submissions. Back in 1921, Sir Roland St. John Braddell,[5] scholar-lawyer had stated that "the plain unvarnished fact that governs the whole matter is that the views of the Chinese of this Colony are so very divergent that legislation is practically impossible" (Braddell 1921, p. 165). However in his evidence before the 1926

Committee, he had apparently changed his stance somewhat. Addressing the Committee, Sir Roland accused the Straits Settlements colonial authorities of being behind other colonial territories in having "let things slide" (CMC 1926, p. 153). Hong Kong had "taken the bull by the horns" (CMC 1926, p.153) and had, as had the Federated Malay States, enacted marriage and family regulations which followed Chinese customary law more closely (CMC 1926, p. 153). Sir Roland personally recalled that during the previous twenty years, two bills had been prepared (in the Straits Settlements) but that "the divergence of opinion amongst the Chinese caused the Attorney General to drop the matter" (CMC 1926, p. 154).

This "divergence of opinion" continued to trammel the colonial efforts represented in the 1926 Chinese Marriage Committee.[6] Oral evidence was taken from forty-four persons — of whom nineteen were women, Sir Roland Braddell being the only non-Chinese. Of the 155 written submissions received, "practically all were from Chinese ladies in Penang" (CMC 1926, p. 3). No explanation of this phenomenon is offered, but elsewhere in the Commitee Report mention is made of the Penang Chinese Ladies Chin Woo (Athletic) Association, of which one of the ladies who gave evidence was the president, and another the secretary. The association's title perhaps suggests a rather more dashing spirit of modernity than the Chinese Ladies Association, already well established in Singapore.

Except for "a limited number of gentlemen of advanced views" (CMC 1926, p. 4), men expressed discomfort with the idea of registering marriage and almost all were opposed to any government intervention. The fears expressed suggest that this was seen as a thin end of the wedge towards the banning of polygamy.

From the women, the Committee heard a unanimous desire for registration of marriage to protect the family from problems arising from concubinage. "Only one legal wife should get the estate" (CMC 1926, p. 149). In addition, one widowed lady described the great difficulty she had experienced in proving her status when she sought an issue of Letters of Administration after her husband's death (CMC 1926, p. 87).

In the discussion of divorce, the women were unanimous on a man's right to divorce an unfaithful wife. But they all expressed a somewhat diffident attitude in relation to an unfaithful husband's behaviour. "If a man misbehaves but treats his wife well, he should not be divorced" (CMC 1926, p. 88); "Taking a mistress should not be a grounds for divorce, unless he ill-treats his wife" (CMC 1926, p. 148); a woman "should be lenient and give the man more chances" (CMC 1926, p. 155); moreover, "If there is adultery by the man it cannot be helped" (CMC 1926, p. 146). There were many more statements along the same lines. Clearly recreational infidelity was either not greatly objected to, or was accepted as merely one of the "c'est la vie" aspects of married life. The emotional tone of these answers is hard to judge, but the strength of women's opposition to relationships resulting in polygamous families comes through loud and clear.

Men on the whole opposed the idea of divorce, which was seen as unnecessary as long as secondary marriages were permitted. One man witness, when asked how he could be so adamant in his opposition to divorce, as it was by then permitted under the civil law of the Republic of China, replied that he did not accept this "because the Chinese Republic is in the hands of Christians" (CMC 1926, p. 69), reflecting an interesting take on political developments in the Far East. This view is all the more interesting because it was expressed at a time when the Communists were still in alliance with the Nationalist/ Kuomintang Party in China (and still, therefore, influential). It was the 1927 split that left the right wing (with Christian connections) in power.

It is hardly surprising then, that the Committee made only very modest recommendations for change — mainly for a system of voluntary registration. "In the present state of public opinion there is no such general desire for facilities for divorce, even among British subjects of Chinese descent, as would justify legislation" (CMC 1926, p. 4). Modest recommendations and an even more modest follow-up; the colonial government once more let matters slide, and customary practices were left to carry on. It was business as usual.

The Women's Charter Takes Shape

And "business went on as usual" until 1961. The Women's Charter was the "great divide" in Singapore family law. It mandated one statutory, indisputable, basis for all non-Muslim marriages, and required that these marriages be monogamous. It also provided for the protection of young women and girls. In the words of one member of the Legislative Assembly, Dr Lee Siew Choh, it was "essentially a women's Bill of Rights" (SLAD 12, 1960, p. 454).

The family provisions were based in general outline on the 1940 Civil Marriage Ordinance, but had involved "urgent work by the legal draftsmen of the Attorney-General's Chambers, searching for precedents in the legislation of other countries" (Lee 1998, p. 326).[7]

The Civil Marriage Ordinance had allowed marriage where one party was Muslim. This clause was dropped, but later restored in a 1967 amendment. Also amended was an error which I recall as causing some hilarity in the local Bar, and which was seen as evidence of the deadline pressure under which the original drafting had taken place. The senior draftsman had both a first class honours degree from Cambridge and great respect from his legal confreres for work of a high standard; it was felt that he could only have erred if working within an overtight time-frame. But whatever the reason, the error was there. As appropriate for family law, initially the Charter stated that it applied only to residents of Singapore. But this failed to take into account the anti-vice content of what was then Part X. As a result, the courts were forced to acquit a man charged with running a brothel — in Guillemard Road as I recall — since he was able to claim that he lived and was domiciled in Johor and, therefore, the Charter did not apply to him.[8]

Legislative Assembly Debates and Select Committees, 1960–61

The passing into law of the Charter required both the 1960 and 1961 Legislative Assembly Debates, and the work of Select Committees in both these years. In both sessions, the

Assembly expressed unanimous support for the principle
of monogamous marriage. Indeed one Muslim member,
Hj Yaacob bin Mohd, quoted the holy Qur'an, indicating
that this was also the preferred pattern of marriage in Islam
(SLAD 12, 1960, p. 463).

While supporting monogamy, opposition members were
not satisfied with the Charter. For them, the legislation
did not do enough "to be worthy of the title, the Women's
Charter should uplift in all fields, political, economic,
social, legal, civil, educational and professional ... The
Charter does not help women in relation to discriminatory
salary schemes" (SLAD 12, 1960, p. 445, Mrs Seow Peck
Leng). Indeed later in the debate, PAP chairman Dr Toh
Chin Chye agreed that women were only truly secure if
economically independent (SLAD 12, 1960, p. 470). The
bill did nothing to prevent men from keeping mistresses:
"What a bluff!" — said Tun Lim Yew Hock, leader of
the opposition (SLAD 12, 1960, p. 473). His comment
drew the rejoinder that during his term of office, nothing
whatsoever had been achieved in the way of legislation
to improve the status of women. Minister Byrne took
all comments in his stride; the bill was not perfect, "but
we are trying hard to do something for the people of
Singapore" (SLAD 12, 1960, p. 490).

Some comments from the only opposition woman
member, Mrs Seow Peck Leng, seemed rather at odds with
her role as a modern woman activist. The bill made it an
offence to "use threat or force" to either prevent or bring
about a marriage. She felt that it was "a mother's right",
"a human right" to threaten to disown a daughter aged
over twenty if she intended to marry someone of whom

the mother disapproved (SLAD 12, 1960, p. 449). She also implied her disapproval of the law that women who had become second wives, before the operative date of the Charter, would retain the legal rights to intestate inheritance (SLAD 12, 1960, p. 444).

One Singaporean who wrote in to the 1960 Select Committee saw the Charter as unrelated to women, but as part of the Government's overarching plan to join Malaysia (written submission No. 15 — in Mandarin, Report of the Select Committee [RSC] 1960). By depriving the Chinese of polygamy, the real objective of the Charter was to encourage the Chinese to convert to Islam since a higher percentage of Muslims in the Singapore population would make it much easier for the government to negotiate acceptance into Malaysia.

By the 1961 debate, the government could claim indications of strong support from the community at large. Minister Byrne reported to the 1961 session that in the thirteen months since the 1960 debate "there have been more marriages solemnized in the Registry of Marriages than there had been in the last six years" (SLAD 14, 1961, p. 1216).

Had the Minister followed this up, he would have found that the average age of the couples married in that period was somewhat higher than usual. From those in my own social circle and from hearsay, I learned that a number of middle-class couples who had been married with only fragmentary formalities during the 1942–45 Japanese Occupation thought it fit to regularize their unions under the existing Civil Marriage Ordinance. There was some alarm that if called upon to register under the new Women's

Charter, their marriages might have been declared invalid for not complying with traditional custom.

The couples concerned need not have feared. The major amendment between 1960 and 1961 was the dropping of the requirement that all pre-existing customary marriages, primary or secondary, be registered within a year of the Charter coming into effect.

In the 1960 debate, the most serious concern expressed by opposition members had been related to the (transitional) clause 166 requiring this registration. Critics had seen this as an unnecessary hardship for old couples; even if the fee were modest, this would be a hardship also for the poor. How could the large numbers required to register be accommodated? Also this would be significant only for those who needed to establish a claim to property whereas in reality, there was no property to be claimed in most marriages. The 1960 Select Committee also received/heard many written and oral anxieties about the requirement that pre-existing marriages must be registered.

Registration was indeed intended to protect the property interests of women by establishing their married status beyond doubt. But opposition members and Select Committee witnesses failed to recognize that it was also intended to facilitate regularized divorce among those previously married by customary rites. Also, registration would prevent a man already married by custom prior to the coming into force of the Charter from claiming to be a bachelor later and contracting a further marriage under the new monogamous legislation.

Perhaps it was the daunting logistics of registering several hundred thousand marriages, and recognition of the problems of the old and poor which led to the dropping of the requirement. As things turned out, perhaps the number of spurious bachelors who abused the system was also small. But social workers were aware of their existence. Two such cases for which my recollections can vouch, were in the farming areas that were still widespread around the island then: the wife of the customary marriage living on the farm, the husband and the "Women's Charter wife" enjoying the benefits of a Housing Development Board (HDB) flat.

The Women's Charter on the Statute Book

By 15 September 1961, the Women's Charter was in the statute book. Legally recognized, monogamous marriage by registration from then on applied to all non-Muslim Singaporeans. Religious officiators could be designated as deputy registrars so that the needs of members of other religions were also met. This represented a radical legal change, but not everything changed and not straightaway.

Yeh Hwa-Kuo (1969) made a detailed study of 50 per cent of all marriages registered in 1962, a sample of 2,252, of whom 1,342 couples were interviewed. He notes that the registrar confirmed his observation that "residents living in outlying villages, and the illiterate" were markedly under-represented in his sample (Yeh 1969, p. 38). Apparently those beyond the reach of the media still continued to marry in the customary style. A 1967 humane and benevolent amendment of the Charter regularized their situation — and at the same time also slammed the door tight shut on any future failures to observe the law.

Nor did views on what constituted a socially recognized marriage undergo universal or radical change. A registry marriage is still regarded by many as if it were merely a legally binding engagement, but not marriage. In the eyes of the couple and their respective families, the marriage is only socially recognized after the tea ceremony and a dinner. The HDB is quite comfortable with the registration stage, and hands over the keys of the flat for which the couple had been queuing since declaring themselves engaged. But it would not yet be respectable for them to live in their flat, although they are free to play "Wendy-houses", unchaperoned and to make all the preparations for taking up residence later on. But should a pregnancy occur at this stage, panic all round, and dinner arrangements hastily brought forward from the date originally planned. Someone has commented that Singapore must be the only country in the world which requires a restaurateur to legitimize a birth.

While legally dead and buried, socially-recognized secondary unions are still with us — the women and children from these unions, however, have scant legal protection. The study of obituaries in the *Straits Times* — a rich source of information on many interesting trends — occasionally lists a second wife, where the age of the deceased makes it unlikely that he was polygamous by 15 September 1961. In conversation and even quite recently in certain official reports, a man may be referred to as having a second wife. Provided the father recognizes the children of such a union as his, they carry a social legitimacy. He may provide for them in his will, but they would be left unprotected if he died intestate.

The Women's Charter — Anti-vice Legislation Together with Family Law?

While monogamous marriage, divorce, and other related issues constituted the "meat" of the Charter, there was another facet. It is an old joke, but one too good to resist repeating. When the Women's Charter, Ordinance No. 18 of 1961, burst upon everyone in all its radical glory, it was unique and non-pareil in being the only piece of major family legislation which not only defines a brothel, but does so on line 6.[9]

Nor was this inappropriate. Parts I through IX of the Charter comprised family law and dealt with such matters as marriage, divorce, and maintenance of wives and children. In contrast, the then Part X provided for the protection of young women and girls from prostitution, and the criminalizing of all third party profiteers who preyed on their earnings.

In any piece of legislation, it is standard practice that the introductory list of definitions of terms used therein should cover the whole statute, and in alphabetical order. It is rather unfortunate in this case that the word "brothel" happens to start with the letter "b".

Was it really necessary to have the "b" word leering at us on that first page? In the 1960 Legislative Assembly Debate, the opposition thought not: "lumping wives together with prostitutes", snorted Tun Lim Yew Hock (SLAD 12, 1960, p. 471). Although in much more measured tones, the 1973 Committee to Review the Women's Charter (of which I was a member), rather agreed with him. The Committee recommended that the Charter should be renamed the

Family Law Act. With some tweaking, the Children and Young Persons Act (CYPA) could raise the age limit of "Young Persons" to extend the necessary protection to girls older than the current limit of sixteen years. Procurers and others profiting from "immoral earnings" could then be dumped into the Penal Code, where they properly belonged. But following the submission of the Committee's report, the name of the Charter remained as it was — and in fact as it still is to this day.

If we look to reason or disembodied logic for this structure of the Charter, we find no answers. The then Part X was in no way radical, or even new. It more or less replicated exactly the old colonial Women and Girls' Protection Ordinance, originally a rather feeble protective piece of legislation, dating from 1887. Via a long string of amendments, each increasing the power to protect girls and penalize more effectively those who preyed on their earnings, the Ordinance was by 1930 compatible with the League of Nations (and later the United Nations) standards. It was also in line with the internationally sanctioned approach of dealing with prostitution by "abolition", and not by licensing or prohibition — the latter two approaches being seen as harmful to women in the long run (United Nations 1959). The most major change in the Charter Part X was to raise the age up to which a girl (deemed to be in "moral danger") could be detained against her will, from 18 to 21 — hardly a complicated amendment.

How do we explain both the political euphoria surrounding the launching of the Women's Charter and this combination of family and anti-vice measures in one legal instrument? For some understanding, we need to look at the political circumstances of Singapore's independence movement and to recall the heady days before and around the 1959 General Election. We also need to look at the respective political roles of English- and Chinese-educated women at that time.

Women Working For Change

English-educated Singapore women did not have a tradition of political activism. Among the post-war group living in exile because of their anti-colonial proclivities — John Eber, Lim Hong Bee, P.V. Sharma — the only Singapore woman, to my knowledge, was Mrs Eber (Tan 2007).[10] The politically radical Malayan Democratic Union (1945–48) apparently had almost exclusively male Singapore members.

Women's groups which attracted the English-educated, such as the long established Chinese Ladies Association and the Young Women's Christian Association (YWCA), and the more recent Kamala Club and Young Women's Muslim Association, were focused on service, welfare, education, and fund-raising for "good causes". Women were also active in western-style organizations such as the Family Planning Association (1949), the Singapore Children's Society (1952), and a whole range of associations initiated after World War II and devoted to the needs of those with disabilities. While all sought progress in their respective fields, none was focused on radical political change. In the words of one of the most able of the civically active, women could achieve most through service "rather than by fighting for one's rights" (Chew 1999, p. 8ff).[11]

Earlier, relatively non-radical political parties did attract a small number of English-educated women members — some very able. But when the PAP began to campaign in earnest in the run up to the 1959 General Election, there appeared to have been few English-educated women members.[12] In his memoirs, Lee Kuan Yew wrote of the great difficulty in finding even one English-educated woman capable of making a party political broadcast. Interestingly, he did not refer to auditioning women members, but "candidates' wives". Eventually, it was Mrs Lee Kuan Yew who had to make the speech (Lee 1998, p. 325).

Although, as outcomes tended to show, English-educated women failed to get the full message, they were introduced to a whole new lexicon of activism in the 1950s, with the arrival of one of the great women of twentieth-century India, Mrs Shirin Fozdar. She accompanied her husband to Singapore when he moved here to practise medicine.

Mrs Fozdar had grown up and been socialized in the seething Indian independence movement and had been personally called upon by Mahatma Gandhi to help settle a major intercommunal outbreak. At age twenty-nine, she had represented an all-Asia women's organization at a League of Nations meeting in Geneva.[13] A study of anti-colonialism in India shows that in that country, Mrs Fozdar was one of many such women (Kaur 1968; Lebra 2008). In Singapore, she was unique. It may sound a little cruel to say so, but in terms of radical political awareness, she was virtually "an Atlantic salmon landing among rather small riverine trout". Mrs Seow Peck Leng, who prided herself in being in the forefront of action by women, regretted that: "Mrs Fozdar's ideas were too radical even for me" (Chew 1999, p. 5ff).

Becoming aware of the vulnerability of Singaporean women in the family context, and aided in raising public consciousness by a visit from Mrs Sutan Shahrir (who was politically prominent in newly-independent Indonesia) in November 1951, Mrs Fozdar organized a public meeting. The meeting, which was well attended, included four women members of the legislative and municipal councils. The meeting agreed on the need to "ameliorate the legal disabilities" (Chew 1999, p. 4) that women suffered; and on the founding of the Singapore Council of Women (SCW), modelled on the National Council of Women in India (Chew 1999, p. 4). Mrs Fozdar was elected secretary — the powerful role much favoured by the politically discerning.

Under her leadership, the council gained much local publicity for its mission and forged a truly formidable range of international links, which reflected Mrs Fozdar's level of energy and experience in activism. By 1954, the council had drafted and distributed to the Legislative Council members a draft Prevention of Bigamous Marriages Bill (Chew 1999, p. 11). This draft received initial support from two members, interestingly neither of them Chinese. It was dropped because of strong opposition from members of the Hindu community, who, disproportionate to their numbers, were politically significant in the early 1950s (Lee 1998, p. 140).

Mrs Fozdar had a flair for achieving publicity for her council and for making statements to the press which tended to unnerve some concerned but less "politically educated" women who might otherwise have been her able supporters. Her most memorable and most hellraising effort was the time she stepped off the plane on her return from an international meeting and announced to the assembled

press that "Singapore is one big brothel". The paparazzi
lapped this up: the colonial rearguard establishment was
not amused.[14]

In terms of her strategies, Mrs Fozdar was ahead of
her time, which perhaps gave strength to the Singapore
Women's Association (SWA), founded in 1957 by Singapore
Democratic Party member of the Legislative Council, Mrs
Seow Peck Leng. SWA stood for monogamy and equal
pay for equal work, but Mrs Seow's party did not get
these issues onto the Legislative Council agenda. Like
Mrs Fozdar, Mrs Seow also gained international standing,
holding office in the Pan Pacific South East Asian Women's
Association. After the 1959 General Election, she was the
only non-PAP woman member of the (by then) Legislative
Assembly and, indeed, the only English-educated woman
member in Chamber.

Mrs Seow was a fine speaker and an able organizer,
but lacked the radical vision of the modern woman which
Mrs Fozdar understood so well. This was reflected in a
contribution she made as a member of the Select Committee
1960. One clause of the Women's Charter Bill referred
to the right of a married woman to pursue a career. Mrs
Seow questioned whether it was "wicked or bad" if a rich
family, amply able to support a daughter-in-law, sought
to prevent the younger woman from working if they felt
her doing so damaged their social prestige (RSC 1960,
p. B73). History does not record Mrs Fozdar's comments
when (and if) this contribution to the discourse on women's
progress reached her ears.

When the time came for representations to be made
to the Select Committee on the Women's Charter in May

1960, it was (quite properly) the President of SCW, Mrs Lee Cheng Hiong, who attended in person and not Mrs Fozdar, the secretary. The performance of the president — the only woman witness to address the committee — was, alas, not impressive (RSC 1960, Appendix II, pp. B1–B15, paras. 1–109). She focused mainly on one point (and at great length) — that the Charter should be retroactive and deprive pre-existing "concubines" (she insisted on this word) and their children of inheritance rights (RSC 1960, paras. 1–99). The Speaker of the House who chaired the Select Committee clarified that it had been legal for a man to have more than one wife: "we do not have the phrase 'more than one wife' in our vocabulary" (RSC 1960, para. 40) and "those whom God has put together let no man put asunder" (RSC 1960, para. 42) — an oddly Book of Common Prayer angle on Chinese customary marriage.

The Speaker pressed the point that the objective was to protect all women, including the already recognized secondary wives. After another forty paragraphs of argument came: "They have had the legal rights before. Now the Singapore Women's Council would like to take away these legal rights, and I think that should be so" (RSC 1960, para. 82). The Speaker could not accept this, but after a further seventeen paragraphs opined that "we are going round in circles" (RSC 1960, para. 99).

The SCW President also stated that she did not trust judges: "sometimes they misjudge too", and that "there should be a board or a body of people representative of the public of Singapore to decide on the custody of children in divorce cases" (RSC 1960, paras. 101–8).

The written representation from the Council suggests that this had been written by a clearer and abler mind, but the oral representation could not have left a favourable impression on any present at that meeting of the Select Committee. Politically, English-educated women still had far to go in understanding even the position of women as a whole.

The political fervour of the Chinese-educated was something quite different and had descended on post-war Singapore like a tsunami of anti-colonial activism, following seismic changes in China in 1949. Those who were around during those years will never forget the impact this had on daily life and civil order at that time. Chinese-educated women — Nanyang University and high school students, as well as factory workers — were as totally involved as the men. They were imbued with total belief in the rightness of all that the New China stood for and were as determined as any evangelist to spread the gospel of their belief, by violence, if necessary.

Unlike the English-educated, those from Chinese schools had benefited little from colonial rule. The Chinese high school equivalent of an "O" levels got you a job as a bus conductor. The Hock Lee Bus Company riots bore witness to the bitterness and frustration, providing tinder for the Communist torch (Lee 1998).

This period has been much written about and Lee Kuan Yew's *The Singapore Story* documents the struggle, touch-and-go at times, to divert this pro-Communist fervour into nationalist channels. This fervour included admiration for the reformed Marriage Law in Mao's China and for the "anti yellow culture" struggles waged there. "Yellow culture" denoted "all the decadent and degenerate behaviour that had brought China to its knees in the 19th century" (Lee 1998, p. 326), which included concubinage and prostitution. It was necessary for the new government to "outflank the Communists with puritanical zeal" (Lee 1998, p. 326). "We rely on the Chinese-educated when we go for elections", reiterated Lee Kuan Yew (Tan 1999, p. 77).

Perhaps we can attribute the presentation to this fervent electorate of monogamous marriage and the suppression of vice in one great Women's Charter to just this political exigency. The English-educated PAP leadership of the time had to tread warily lest they be seen to have colonial attachments; the Women and Girls' Protection Ordinance, intrinsically neutral, had very definite colonial attachments and, as such, just would not do.

Reluctance to change the structure, more than a decade later and with a very different political scenario now, is harder to explain — perhaps it is because of a powerful nostalgia for the days of struggle, cliff-hanging, and hard-won triumph?

Conclusion

Was the PAP ideologically committed to the Women's Charter, or was this item in its manifesto a response to pressures from the passionately puritan electorate? Almost certainly it was both.

Through the company they had kept during their periods of overseas education, the leaders in the party had been intensively exposed to the values of modern social democracies. Membership of this fraternity of modern nations was what they aspired to for their own independent country. It is inconceivable that they would expect to drag into this membership a vaguely defined system of polygamous customary marriage with distinctly sleazy outer fringes. Once the improved status of women is accepted as a hallmark of modernity (and as a prerequisite for economic development), then monogamous marriage becomes axiomatic.

In their growing-up years, these leaders had been (like the rest of us) exposed to the age-old values of their forebears. As we mature and experience a wider world, we come to question, and on the level of cognition, reject aspects of the ancestral baggage which we interpret as inappropriate for our own age. But these old values that we reject tend to linger on in the psyche.

There is perhaps evidence of this lingering among some members of the PAP leadership. From the "Men in White" has emerged an incident in which Madam Miki Goh, seen as politically unreliable, was ejected from the inner circle of the early (1954) PAP planning stage, protesting strongly on her way out.[15] What is interesting is not the rights and wrongs of Madam Goh's individual case, but the consequence — thereafter *all* women were excluded, including the very able Mrs Lee Kuan Yew, whose political credentials were impeccable, and who indeed appealed against her own exclusion. It would seem that the PAP did not treat Madam Goh merely as one troublesome individual: she was a woman — and if one woman is troublesome, their conclusion was to exclude all women. It was only in the 1957 election to the party's Central Executive Committee (CEC) that two women were brought into the inner circle

— both Chinese-educated, representing powerful voting potential for a general election already on the horizon.

It seemed that values from the past also came up in the 1980s. Then Prime Minister Lee Kuan Yew spoke of his anxieties regarding trends in patterns of marriage and fertility at the time. As if thinking aloud, he asked if perhaps his party had been too hasty in launching the Women's Charter. Perhaps it was a loss that Singapore no longer had the polygamous and upwardly mobile businessman passing on his Darwinianly valuable genes through his multiple families.

In response to the Prime Minister's uttering of these retrograde thoughts, women's groups sprang into action — "Women's Charter — YES; Polygamy — NO" declared the blazing red T-shirts of the Association of Women for Action and Research (AWARE) members.

And the then Prime Minister received from his own family circle similar, if not more politely expressed messages. Any thinking listener must have recognized this rhetorical question as nostalgia about a past system, and as little more than that. There was simply no alternative to the well thought through path which had been taken.

The process of giving up ancestral values can trail whiffs of past ways in its wake. "Mrs Fozdar? We didn't need her lot, we had our own lunatic lady fringe" — this from one very senior leader on a social occasion at which an unwary speaker was attributing the Women's Charter to Mrs Fozdar's goodly efforts. It was said with a kindly, if quizzical, smile, but was hardly the utterance of a "born again" believer in the total equality of men and women.

International women's groups, mainly anglophone, have tended to take special note of the role of Mrs Fozdar, the SCW, and related groups, and to have viewed the Women's Charter as a culmination of their efforts. The women involved did indeed work tremendously hard to raise consciousness, but in terms of influencing the PAP manifesto for the 1959 General Election, the English-educated as a whole were politically non-starters.

With few exceptions, the English-educated failed to understand that the "right-wing" of the PAP was waging a desperate struggle to divert communist fervour into nationalist channels. They also did not recognize the strategies that this involved. In previous elections, only British citizens (predominantly Indian, Eurasian, and Straits-born Chinese) had been eligible to vote. The creation of Singapore citizenship in 1958 enfranchised the mass of the Chinese population, and politics would never be the same again. Of this, the PAP leadership was well aware; in 1959, only the Chinese-educated voter could sweep them to power — and to this electorate policies must appeal.

And in order to appeal, those policies must resonate with some of the values of the model which, for the Chinese at that time, represented political excellence — the regime under which China had "stood up", and under which (among other things) had been purified of "yellow culture". At far remove indeed, but perhaps the Women's Charter owed less to Mrs Fozdar and more to Chairman Mao.

Epilogue

It is interesting to note that several of those who gave evidence at the Select Committee stage made recommendations well ahead of their times. In summary, these were proposals for incorporating protection from family violence into the Charter (RSC 1960, p. B69) and making some provision for the care of old parents (RSC 1960, p. A69).

The proposal to incorporate rights to care by old people was dismissed as a family matter. Decades later, this issue was to become a basis for legislation, in the Maintenance of Parents Act of 1996.

The Select Committee witness who pleaded for specific protections for victims of family violence to be written into the Charter was told that those with problems should approach the Department of Social Welfare. Minister Byrne assured the witness that while in colonial times the Counselling and Advice Section (CAS) of the Department "had officials who were the pro-*towkay* type", it was now staffed by "Chinese educated women" (RSC 1960, pp. B70 and 72). While the Minister may have been right in respect of an occasional corrupt individual, on the basis of personal experience, I would beg to differ strongly with this view of times past. I recall that CAS staff, even in the early 1950s, had included several able "Chinese-educated women" of impeccable integrity.

Following the activism of Nominated Member of Parliament, Dr Kanwaljit Soin, the Women's Charter was amended in 1996 to include greatly enhanced powers to deal with family violence. Let us hope that the Select Committee witness, who pleaded for this enhancement back in 1960, lived to see his recommendation become law.

Addendum: A Brief Note on Law in Relation to Muslim Women[16]

What of the Muslim woman? At the time her sisters of other faiths (or no faith) were receiving their "bill of rights" in the form of the Women's Charter, how was she faring? For her "a great leap forward" had come earlier, when the Syariah Court was finally up and running in November 1958.

The form of, and the rules governing, Muslim marriages had been laid down legally since the Mohammedan Marriage Ordinance No. 5 of 1880, which provided for the voluntary registration of both past and future marriages and divorces. Even when a 1908 Amendment made registration compulsory, this also stated that failure to register, while an offence, did not invalidate either a marriage or a divorce.

Judith Djamour (1959, p. 141) notes that by 1950, women's groups, Muslim leaders, and the Muslim Advisory Board were all expressing concern about the high rate of marital breakdown among Muslims in Singapore. In 1951, an official committee was set up to seek reforms, but it was not until 1957 that the relatively progressive Muslims Ordinance (No. 25 of 1957) was passed into law "to repeal and re-enact the law relating to Muslims, the registration of marriages and divorces and to establish the Syariah Court". The time it took for this to happen did not relate to the establishment of the court, on which there was consensus, but to clauses relating to wills and inheritance.

I recall personally, from my mid-1950s employment in the Department of Social Welfare, that during that period of gestation, social workers faced many problems in their efforts to help Muslim women in distress. In the absence of a Muslim Court, there was no official body to which we could look for advice.

Sometimes the problem was post-divorce disputes about who rightfully owned what. In those days, the neighbourhood *kadi* (the registrar of Muslim marriages and divorces) was often ill-educated himself and relied on marriage and divorce fees as a major source of livelihood. Women were quick to make accusations of petty corruption, claiming, for example, that for a few dollars "under the table" the *kadi* had declared her precious sewing machine (bought out of her savings) to be the property of her husband. Where the said machine was her best source of income, this was no small matter for the poor woman. Yet there was virtually nothing we could do to help her as there was no Legal Aid Bureau, no Small Claims Court, and no religious authority to whom we could refer the woman for help.

Sometimes the problem was related to the interventions made by the Department of Social Welfare to alleviate her plight. If the only job available for an illiterate Muslim woman involved washing dishes in the "non-halal" kitchen of a non-Muslim family, would we be placing her in a position of sin in the eyes of her community? Our Muslim colleagues (always the first to be consulted) often felt inadequately schooled to make a decision. We flailed about using our personal resources — a friend in the Malay Studies Department at the then University of Malaya (but only a few of them felt able to discuss a matter involving Muslim law). Or we sought help from an approachable Muslim member of the Bar (but not all of them had studied Islamic law as well as secular law).[17]

The 1957 Ordinance did not give women all the protection they needed, but the Syariah Court and related regulations took care of many of the injustices that had arisen under the old and outdated system. An amendment of 1960 limited power to register a polygamous marriage to the Chief *kadi* only. The locality *kadi* could no longer register a divorce unless it was by mutual consent. All contested divorces — and disputes over "sewing machines" — now came before the court. Djamour's close study of proceedings (Djamour 1966) — she was literate in both romanized Malay and Jawi — indicated that the staff made every effort to protect the interests of those whose cases were heard.

Maintenance matters were still handled by the secular courts, but the Administration of Muslim Law Act No. 27 of 1966 raised the status of the Syariah Court and widened its jurisdiction.

Notes

1. See "The Way Ahead: A Five Year Plan" (Singapore: Petir, 1958).
2. By 1955, India had introduced monogamous marriage legislation. As gathered from interviews conducted in the 1990s, before that time the customary law of different Hindu traditions and regions had varied in the degree to

which polygamy had been an accepted practice. However, the 1955 legislation did not always percolate down to the village level. The parents of a Singapore-born Indian girl used to worry when their immigrant son-in-law paid a visit alone to his family back in India, especially if his wife in Singapore belonged to an unrelated family. In a culture which favoured marriage between cousins, he could face pressure back in the village to marry a girl from within the kin group. By Singapore standards, he might be a man of modest means, but in the eyes of the villagers he was a most eligible match, and it was desired to keep the fruit of his overseas labour within the family circle.

3. Derived from combining figures for "married", "widowed", and "divorced", on pages 125 and 127 of the 1957 Census Report.

4. Freedman (1952) noted that he came across only one such marriage between two teachers in Chinese schools. The link with the May 4th Movement came to me as a personal communication, also from a teacher in a Chinese school.

5. Sir Roland St. John Braddell was described by the Chair of the Chinese Marriage Committee as having "made a special study ... of the legal position of Chinese marriages in the Colony" (CMC 1926, p. 150).

6. Originally, the Committee comprised twelve men. Within a few months, the names of three women were added. Two are named as the wives of prominent citizens, along with Dr Lee, the first local woman graduate of the King Edward VII Medical School.

7. See Chapter 3 in this volume.

8. Personal recollections of lawyers' conversations.

9. The writer was assured by lawyers that no other country combines family and anti-vice measures in one statute (personal communication).

10. The wives of the other two exiles listed are remembered for their long and distinguished careers in the Singapore Medical Service.

11. Interestingly, a 1930s generation of English-educated Chinese women had gone to great lengths and made great personal sacrifices to collect funds to finance the battles to stem Japan's incursions into China. In 1943, Indian women flocked to join the Rani of Jhansi Regiment of the Indian National Army (Lebra 2008), ready to fight and die beside their brothers for the liberation of India from colonial rule. For neither was Singapore yet quite their spiritual home.

12. English-educated women supporters in the civil service were precluded by their employment status from joining a political party.

13. See Chew (1999) for a full and scholarly account of Mrs Fozdar's impact on the organization of women in Singapore.

14. I am quoting vivid personal recollections of this incident and the subsequent hullabaloo.

15. Mrs Phillip Hoalim Jnr., otherwise known by her maiden name, Madam Miki Goh (whose official name was Wembley Goh, as she was born in 1923, the year of that great Exhibition), was my closest friend during my last year at the London School of Economics (1949–50). She belonged to a lineage of strong women, being niece to Miss Lim Beng Hong (Mrs B.H. Oon), the first woman to be admitted to the Bar in Singapore and Malaya. Miki was a generous and deeply caring person, ready to fight for what she believed in. I do not for one moment believe she was a committed Communist, but she could be impulsive.

16. It must be emphasized that this is not a full account of the legal situation, which is beyond the scope of the present chapter.

17. I recall with warm gratitude the many occasions in which I received wise counsel from the late and generous Mr M.J. Namazie, senior member of the Bar, and recognized "elder" in the Muslim community; also from Professor Fatimi, mid-1950s visiting professor at the Department of Malay Studies, (then) University of Malaya.

References

Braddell, Roland St. J. "Chinese Marriages as regarded by the Supreme Court of the Straits Settlements". *Journal of the Straits Branch of the Royal Asiatic Society* 83 (1921): 153–65.

Chew, Phyllis. *The Singapore Council of Women and the Women's Movement*. Singapore: AWARE Publication, 1999.

Djamour, Judith. *The Muslim Matrimonial Court in Singapore*. London: University of London, Athlone Press, 1966.

————. *Malay Kinship and Marriage in Singapore*. London: University of London, Athlone Press, 1959.

Freedman, Maurice. *Chinese Family and Marriage in Singapore*. London: HMSO, 1957.

————. "Colonial Law and Chinese Society". *Journal of the Royal Anthropological Institute* LXXX (1952): 97–126.

Kaur, Manmoham. *Role of Women in the Freedom Movement, 1857–1947*. Delhi: Sterling Publications, 1968.

Lebra, Joyce C. *Women Against the Raj: The Rani of Jhansi Regiment*. Singapore: Institute of Southeast Asian Studies, 2008.

Lee Kuan Yew. *The Singapore Story*. Singapore: SPH Times Editions, 1998.

Purcell, Victor. *The Chinese in Malaya*. London: Oxford University Press, 1968.

Song Ong Siang. *One Hundred Years of the Chinese in Singapore*. London: John Murray, 1923.

Tan, Kevin Y.L. "The Legalists: Kenny Byrne and Eddie Barker". In *Lee's Lieutenants: Singapore's Old Guard*, edited by Lam P.E. and K.Y.L. Tan. St. Leonards, NSW, Australia: Allen & Unwin, 1999.

Tan Siok Sun. *Goh Keng Swee: A Portrait*. Singapore: Didier Millet, 2007.

"The Way Ahead: A Five Year Plan". Singapore: Petir, 1958.

United Nations. *Study on Traffic in Persons and Prostitution*. New York: Department of Economic and Social Affairs, 1959.

Wee, Ann. "The Way We Were". In *The Ties that Bind: In Search of the Modern Singapore Family*. Singapore: AWARE, 1996.

Yeh Hwa-Kuo. "Chinese Marriage in Singapore". Ph.D. dissertation, Department of Sociology, New York University, New York, U.S., 1969.

Legislative Documents

Chinese Marriage Committee (CMC). Report of the proceedings of the committee appointed by the governor to report on matters concerning Chinese marriages. Singapore, 1926.

Chua, S.C. Report of the Census of Population, 1957. Singapore: Government Printer, 1964.

Report of the Select Committee on the Women's Charter Bill. April 1960. Legislative Assembly 16 of 1960 (RSC 1960).

Singapore Legislative Assembly Debates, Vol. 14, May 1961 (SLAD 1961).

————, Vol. 12, 13 January–1 June 1960 (SLAD 1960).

The Women's Charter (Amendment) Act, No. 9 of 1967.

The Women's Charter Bill, No. 81 of 1960.

The Women's Charter Ordinance, No. 18 of 1961.

3
Significant Provisions in the Women's Charter

Leong Wai Kum

The Women's Charter is Chapter 353 of Singapore's statutes.[1] It was originally enacted in 1961 as the common marriage and family statute for non-Muslim Singaporeans.[2] The People's Action Party (PAP) had included as one item in its election manifesto[3] the complete review of Singapore's existing family laws with a view to improving the unsatisfactory state of these laws that were affecting non-Muslim Singaporeans.[4] The statute came into existence when the successful party made good on this promise.

Why the Women's Charter is Noteworthy Even to Non-lawyers

Even to non-lawyers, there are two features of the Women's Charter that make this a statute of note.

Important Tool in National Reconstruction

It is rare to encounter a statute, such as the Women's Charter, the enactment of which by the legislature was so closely bound up with the political development of the nation. The political party that won the first general election to the legislature held in Singapore in 1959, and has remarkably continued its winning streak since then, rightly envisioned national reconstruction to require the efforts of both men and women equally: "[W]e stand for equality ... of opportunity for education and employment for all Singapore citizens."[5] Thus the political leaders wisely believed in raising the status and marital condition of the majority of women:

> Women who form nearly half of our population have an important part to play in our national construction. In the first instance in order to emancipate them from the binds of feudalism and conservatism a monogamous marriage law will be passed.[6]

Indeed the PAP moved the enactment of the Women's Charter[7] in the first session of the First Legislative Assembly of the State of Singapore on 2 March 1960.

Value of giving women equality within their marriage

The enactment of the Women's Charter was thus a momentous event in the relatively short history of Singapore. The leaders rightly reasoned that if Singapore was to be lifted from its fairly low economic status in the late 1950s, when the most profitable sector of the economy was the port of entry of goods bound for the Malayan hinterland, it needed its entire population to be as highly educated and economically productive as possible. Each individual man and woman had to play his or her part. Several initiatives needed to be pursued. Quality education had to be freely accessible. Childcare and health services had to be improved and made accessible to all. Children, the spring source of the nation, had to be valued, and no difference was to be drawn between girls and boys. Both had to be nurtured and educated to the highest level possible. Workers had to be protected and the employment of women encouraged.

In this regard, it became crucial that women be accorded the same rights and protection that men had been enjoying all along. The circumstance where legal equality should expressly be espoused is within marriage. Where the wife is (no more and no less) the equal of the husband, the seeds for the future well-being of children, both sons and daughters, are sown. As the political leaders rightly envisioned, each step in this endeavour brought benefits that were magnified in the successive economic leaps Singapore made towards its current enviable position within the first world of nations.

Change name of statute?

There have been calls to change the name of the statute from the "Women's Charter" to something more reflective of its contents, for example, "Family Law Act". While these calls are reasonable, the writer does not support them precisely because of the point she made above. A "Family Law Act" loses the link with Singapore's national reconstruction around the middle of the last century. The Women's Charter is unique because few statutes, much less those related with the regulation of marriage and the family, share this feature of being high profile in the regeneration of a whole nation. The writer feels it will be unfortunate if future generations of Singaporeans forget why and how this statute came into existence.

It may be more useful to keep the statute's connection to our nation building than to bear a name that is a better reflection of its contents. To those few persons who wrongly accuse the statute of being biased in favour of women simply because it is named the "Women's Charter", the writer's response is:

> Read the statute and you will find that largely it is gender-neutral. It is neither biased in favour of women nor is it against either men or women. The old common law rules that used to apply here as our basic law at one time negated the legal personality of a woman the moment she became married. It was to correct this anomaly that the Women's Charter required to provide specifically for a married woman to retain all her legal capacities during marriage. In so providing all that the Women's Charter does is to require the family law to treat both married men and married women equally with regard to each person's separate legal personality. Each is returned to his or her full legal status as an individual.

Women's Charter Tells Good Stories of How We View Family Obligations

Family lawyers like to remind us that if we read the law wisely, we see more than legal provisions. The law tells stories about the people it serves. In this regard, the Women's Charter tells stories about us, in particular, how we view the obligations husband and wife owe each other and their children. In most respects, the Women's Charter tells good stories.

The Women's Charter tells that we perceive marriage as "the equal cooperative partnership of different kinds of efforts for the mutual well-being of the spouses". As spouses in a partnership, we aspire to treat each other with equality, discharge our obligations jointly, and generally behave with all reasonable consideration towards each other. As parents, we aspire to cooperate in caring and providing for our children. In economic matters, we trust the courts to make orders that are fair and equitable. Not every aspect of the family law in Singapore is above criticism and there are indeed areas where improvements can easily be made, but it is, by and large, a set of laws that we can all be proud of.

The family law in Singapore, largely through the provisions in the Women's Charter, exhorts moral behaviour and, thereby, teaches us how to be good partners in marriage, and good parents. This chapter highlights some of the core provisions that achieve these laudable goals that any good family law should aspire towards.

Parts of the Women's Charter

As a consolidation of the rules and principles which had been spread over several pieces of legislation, the Women's Charter came to consist of 167 provisions in eleven parts. The current version consists of 186 provisions in twelve parts.

The Women's Charter is at the centre of the non-Muslim marriage and family law in Singapore,[8] although it is still supplemented by several other statutes. Apart from the law in statutes, there are rules and principles that need to be gathered from court decisions. The Women's Charter provisions may be grouped as follows.

Marriage and Its Termination

Seven parts of the statute regulate marriage and its termination. There are provisions on the solemnization and registration of marriages, including the compliance requirements for a valid marriage. Where a marriage is validly solemnized, there is provision that it lasts until one spouse dies, or their union is terminated by a court judgement.

Divorce is rightly offered by the court only as a last resort when it is proven that the marital relationship has irretrievably broken down and there are no facts to suggest that it would be unreasonable for the court to grant the judgement. In ensuring that it is indeed a relief granted only as a last resort, the Women's Charter provisions are aided by procedures put in place by the Family Court in Singapore. When the relationship runs into difficulties, it is social services that should first offer help. The law is too blunt an instrument to help unhappy parties in a marriage mend their relationship. Social services to married persons abound in Singapore. The Family Court in Singapore incorporates the availability of such social services into the information it readily offers married persons who turn to it for help. When all else fails, the law of divorce rightly offers relief.

Husband-wife Relationship

Two parts regulate the relationship that is formed between the husband and wife upon their marriage. The tone of legal regulation is appropriately soft as both spouses are autonomous adults whose right to choose how they shall live with each other should be respected. What the Women's Charter does is to lay down the expectation of reasonable consideration from each of them in the conduct of their relationship. Only gross behaviour, such as threatening violence or actually inflicting violence, is rightly controlled or punished.

Parent-child Relationship

The Women's Charter lays down the fundamental idea that parenthood is a responsibility of parents towards the child which the law will tenaciously hold parents to. This idea sets the right tone for the specifics of legal regulation. In regulating parents and protecting children, the Women's Charter is supplemented by several other statutes in Singapore.

Maintenance and Entitlement to Property

The Women's Charter allows the courts to order a husband to provide reasonable maintenance to his dependent wife, and a parent (or an adult who has accepted a child as a member of his or her family) to provide reasonable maintenance to a dependent child. The courts are also empowered to resolve disputes between family members over their entitlement and use of property that had been purchased by one or both of them.

Financial Reorganization After Divorce

The Women's Charter allows the Family Court, after having awarded the judgement of divorce, to help former spouses achieve fair and reasonable reorganization of their finances. The couple's obligation to continue providing maintenance to their dependent children is, on principle, not at all affected by the divorce, and the Women's Charter conveys this by not making separate provisions of the parents' obligation on their divorce. The point is that the parents' divorce has no effect whatsoever on their continuing parental responsibilities towards their children. While there may have to be court orders regarding with which parent the children should live, these orders do not substitute, or undermine the fundamental idea that both parents still jointly owe the child/children responsibilities.

Reorganization is required of the former spouses' financial obligations between themselves, as well as to ensure that the wealth and property accumulated by both are shared fairly between them. Of the latter, the Women's Charter empowers the court to order the just and equitable division of property determined to be the former spouses' matrimonial assets (generally understood to include all property acquired during the marriage by either or both parties' own efforts). Where this needs to be supplemented, the former husband may still be ordered to continue providing reasonable maintenance to his former wife.

Offences Against Women and Girls

This part of the Women's Charter provides a set of minor offences to supplement other criminal law statutes, specifically, to protect women and girls from vices. It does not sit very well with the rest of the statute and there have been calls to remove it to a more appropriate statute.

Application to Muslim Singaporeans

The extent to which the Women's Charter applies to, and regulates the lives of Muslim Singaporeans, is complex and detailed.[9] A fair summary should start with the premise that Muslim Singaporeans are bound by the same laws as non-Muslim Singaporeans unless there is a statutory provision that exempts them from certain laws and instead allows them the privilege of being regulated by Muslim law. The Muslim law that applies in Singapore consists of the classic religious principles, which are supplemented by provisions in the Administration of Muslim Law Act.[10]

The premise holds within family law as well. The Women's Charter is a general law in Singapore applying to all Singaporeans. Indeed Section 3 of the Women's Charter proclaims that it "shall apply to all persons in Singapore". The only exception appears within its Subsection (2) which provides that the parts of the Women's Charter on the solemnization of marriage and its termination (including the regulation of the relationship between the spouses) shall not apply to a person who is married under Muslim law. The rest of the statute continues to apply.

The legal regulation of the relationship between parents and their children, including their guardianship and custody, applies to all Singaporeans, including Muslim parents and children. The fact that a court will consider the religious affiliation of the Muslim parent while hearing a

custody dispute is not unique to Muslims. The court will
bear a parent's religious affiliation in mind whether it is
Christianity, Hinduism, Islam, Buddhism, Taoism, or any
other faith, as this has an effect on the well-being of the
child concerned. The regulation of a couple's interest in each
other's property while they remain married, as well as the
provision of reasonable maintenance during the course of
marriage, also applies to all Singaporeans, whether Muslim
or non-Muslim. So also does the law protecting each of us
from violence within the family — the law applies across
the board. It is fair to say that Muslim and non-Muslim
Singaporeans are regulated to a greater extent by the same
laws, even within family law, than by laws that are separate
and different.

As the law for divorce is among the few matters where
the Women's Charter provisions do not apply to Muslim
Singaporeans married under Muslim law, it follows that
the law, that empowers the Family Court to order the
just and equitable division of matrimonial assets upon a
couple's divorce, does not apply to a Muslim who has been
divorced according to Muslim law. The Administration of
Muslim Law Act, however, gives the Syariah Court, which
administers the Muslim law of divorce, a similar power
to order the division of matrimonial assets when Muslim
parties divorce.[11] The same is true of the other two powers
that assume importance upon a couple's divorce, namely,
the power of the court to order maintenance for the divorced
wife, and its power to award child custody orders — these
powers in the Women's Charter do not apply to divorced
Muslims, although the Administration of Muslim Law
Act gives similar powers to the Syariah Court.[12] In 1999,

however, by a series of statutory amendments, a Muslim divorced couple is allowed to choose to have their disputes relating to division of matrimonial assets, maintenance, and child custody, transferred to, and heard by, the Family Court instead of by the Syariah Court.[13] With this greater choice to Muslims to choose to be regulated by the general non-Muslim law, the two communities are even more consistently regulated by the same laws administered by the same courts.

Within the fairly large Women's Charter, there are three provisions in particular that deserve close study when we think of the Women's Charter as the repository of societal views of family obligations.

Section 46(1): Message to Spouses — Marriage is Your Equal Cooperative Partnership of Different Efforts

The Women's Charter in its Section 46(1) provides that:

> Upon the solemnization of marriage, the husband and the wife shall be mutually bound to co-operate with each other in safeguarding the interests of the union and in caring and providing for the children.

This is a remarkable provision. It really consists of two separate provisions: one regulating the couple in their behaviour towards each other, and the other regulating them as parents to their children. We begin with the regulation of spouses after noting how Section 46(1) came to be included in the Women's Charter.

Taken from the Swiss Civil Code to Convey Moral Content to the Law

The legislative records reveal that Section 46(1) of the Women's Charter was "taken from the Swiss Civil Code".[14] Very seldom is any part of our law, whether in statute or elsewhere, modelled from law in a civil law country, since Singapore is part of the common law family of legal systems. Countries in Europe (except for England and Wales, as one legal system) belong to the civil law family of legal systems, while the common law family of legal systems is headed by England and includes Singapore, the United States, Australia, and New Zealand.

As if the Women's Charter borrowing from Swiss law is not remarkable enough, the original drafter of the Swiss Civil Code had said this of the reason he wrote the Swiss law the way he did:

> The matrimonial union has moral and legal content. It appears to us desirable to state the moral effects in the law, at least inasmuch as the violations affect the marriage and may possibly provide grounds for divorce.[15]

That the drafter added his personal moral perspective to buttress what were the more technical provisions of the Swiss family laws explains much of the remarkable developments we have made within the family law in Singapore. Much of what is discussed in the following paragraphs may in some way be attributed to this characteristic of conveying moral content in the way our law regulates us as members of our families.

Generations of Singaporeans remain indebted to the wise draftsman of the original Women's Charter in 1961 who chose to model this aspect of our law after the Swiss, thus incorporating a moral message in the legal regulation of spouses. One would be hard put to find another provision such as this within the common law family of legal systems and, indeed, a provision conveying a moral view of marriage may not even be common within codes in the civil law family of legal systems. Suffice it to say that no provision equivalent to our Section 46(1) exists in the core common law countries of England, the United States, Australia, or New Zealand, and the writer firmly believes that their family laws are the poorer for its absence.

Ideal Formulation of Expectations of Married Persons

Section 46(1) of the Women's Charter may well be the ideal formulation of law to express the hopes of general society of every marital union. It clearly supports the continuation of the relationship between husband and wife by saying to them that the law expects each to preserve the relationship with his or her moral commitment towards it. Yet it stops short of directly punishing failure to meet up to its expectations. Some people may criticize it as having no teeth.

The writer disagrees with this portrayal. The characterization of the marital relationship by the Women's Charter Section 46(1) provides optimal legal regulation. The relationship is, it is hoped, of long duration. It is a deep emotional and sexual union. If this intimate relationship is to endure, the parties require utmost privacy to sort out all manner of rights, obligations, responsibilities, and privileges between themselves. Injudicious interference by the law can only cause harm. In this context, the best the law can do is to spell out what the ideal is and leave the parties to achieve it to the best of their abilities.

Marriage, as the equal cooperative partnership of different efforts, provides the right tone in the legal regulation of married couples. Whether the specifics of legal regulation rest on an equally firm moral foundation may be tested by how consistent they are with this view of marriage as the equal cooperative partnership of different efforts. In this regard, the laws in Singapore, regulating a couple's responsibilities as parents, and the courts' exercise of its power to divide their matrimonial assets upon the termination of their marriage, are sound because the defining principles within them convey this view of the nature of marriage to the married couple.

Legal Regulation of Spouses to Conform to Three Characteristics

The legal regulation of the marital relationship, by the tone set in the Women's Charter Section 46(1), should conform with three characteristics:

1. Both husband and wife are expected to behave reasonably towards each other;
2. Both husband and wife owe duties mutually; and
3. Each party retains autonomy in decision-making.

These are the guiding principles. It should be said, though, that not every detail of the law conforms with these principles.

Each principle adds something to the law. Each helps the husband and wife to adjust to marital life and the challenges it poses. Each tells them they owe obligations towards each other. Couples should not forget they share a special relationship. They should do everything they can to protect that relationship and allow it to grow even deeper. It is inevitable that during the course of marriage, one party or the other will fall short. At such times, it is critical for the other party to respond as reasonably as possible. It is equally critical that social services be readily available to assist both of them. Each needs to learn so the two can grow together.

If a couple learns from the guiding principles, their relationship can grow strong enough to withstand all challenges. The proper role of the law in regulating the relationship between the husband and wife is to teach each spouse how to approach his or her relationship with the other, with all the reasonable consideration he or she can muster so that their relationship continues, not just to survive, but also to deepen. The closer the details of the law reflect the delicate balance required by all these guiding principles, the better the law will be.

The amendment to the criminal law to allow a husband to be prosecuted for raping his wife shows how the principles of regulating spouses within family law can influence another area of the law. How should the law of rape apply between husband and wife? At one extreme, the law should be exactly as it applies between two people who are not married to each other. While this appears to offer maximum protection to a wife, we should ask ourselves: Is this perfectly consistent with the obligations that family law reminds her that she has undertaken upon marriage? True, the husband accused of raping his wife has definitely behaved unreasonably towards her. He has fallen far short of what family law teaches him on how he should treat his wife. The husband must learn to behave better and there must be social services readily available in the community to help him learn. If he does, there is a good chance their relationship will continue. If he does not learn, their relationship is headed for the irretrievable breakdown that will give her good reason to divorce him.

But what should a reasonable wife's first response be when a husband is less than considerate in their bedroom? Should she say to her husband: "You are no different from the man who lives next door. If you act towards me the way I would not want our neighbour to, I do not need to consider that you are my husband and I can have you prosecuted for rape." Or should the law encourage a reasonable wife to say, even, to a boorish husband: "You are my husband and we have an intimate relationship that I do not have with our neighbour. That is a significant difference and it affects how the law views your conduct towards me and how it would view our neighbour's conduct if he behaved improperly towards me. Our neighbour commits rape any time he forces his sexual advances on me without my permission. You, my husband, commit rape on me only when our relationship has deteriorated in such a way that you must be even more sensitive to whether or not I welcome your sexual advances. Before our relationship has deteriorated, I shall accord you greater leeway than I do any other man. Once our relationship has deteriorated, however (and you cannot say you did not know this because I have gone to court to obtain a court order, which any reasonable person knows reflects a deterioration in our relationship), you must be very sensitive towards my wishes in the bedroom. If I indicate I do not welcome your sexual advances, you must not insist. If you do, you are a husband who has raped his wife."

The law in Singapore was amended to this latter form of the law of rape as it applies to married couples. Is this the right form? Are both husband and wife treated rightly by the criminal law? Reasonable people can and do disagree regarding what is the best form of the law of rape as it applies to the husband and wife. While she acknowledges the differing view, the writer feels that Singapore's current form of the law bears reasonable consistency with the messages that family law gives.

Legal Regulation Rightly Tempered

The Women's Charter's provisions regulating spouses are appropriately "softer" and less blunt than the common law that existed previously. Except for gross behaviour amounting to violence, there is no punishment of a spouse who fails to live up to the law's expectations. Punishment simply does not work. The law instead cajoles the ideal. Social services must then pick up the baton and offer education and counselling. The law comes back into the picture when these social services are unable to help the couple heal their differences and they pursue the termination of their marriage. Even during divorce court proceedings, the Women's Charter continues to cajole reasonableness from them, and to remind court officials to focus on whether reconciliation may still be possible, and to protect the well-being of children from the worst effects of their parents' problems with each other.

Section 46(1): Message to Parents — You Owe Responsibility Towards Your Child

There is a second moral message within Section 46(1) of the Women's Charter in its concluding words (see p. 89).

Moral View of Parenthood

The provision in Section 46(1) exhorts the equal cooperative efforts of the husband and wife to care and provide for their children. Parenting is as much the equal cooperative partnership of different efforts as the parents' relationship with each other. Indeed, parenting can be considered the pinnacle of cooperation by any two persons. When husband and wife engage in parenting, the Women's Charter creates expectations of them as parents at the same time as it creates expectations of them as spouses to each other. The Women's Charter exhorts parents to adopt a moral view of their parenthood.

Indeed, legal expectations of them as parents are powerful because, not only do they define parenthood in a moral way, they are supplemented by provisions in other statutes that are more directly enforceable in court. There are very important provisions within the Guardianship of Infants Act[16] that direct the courts on how to uphold the well-being of every child whose living arrangement with one or both parents comes to the courts' attention. There is also the Children and Young Persons Act (CYPA)[17] on the public protection of children. Nevertheless, the tone is set by the Women's Charter Section 46(1) which conveys the legal regulation of the relationship between parents and their child through the idea of parents having the responsibility for the care and upbringing of their child.

International Acceptance of Idea of Parental Responsibility

Section 46(1) has existed in the Women's Charter since its original enactment in 1961. It is remarkable to note that the idea of parental responsibility, as opposed to "parental rights", became part of the international legal language only through the United Nations-sponsored Convention of the Rights of the Child in 1989. Article 18 of the Convention requires all countries that have committed to the Convention to:

> use their best efforts to ensure recognition of the principle that both parents have common responsibilities for the upbringing and development of the child. Parents or, as the case may be, legal guardians, have the primary responsibility for the upbringing and development of the child. The best interests of the child will be their basic concern.

It has also been acknowledged in England that the idea of conveying the law through "parental responsibility" only followed the enactment of the UK Children Act 1989. It is remarkable that the Women's Charter in Section 46(1) already conveyed the same idea several decades earlier in 1961.

Affirmation of Responsibility Owed by Potential Parents from Court of Appeal in Singapore

The Court of Appeal in *Lim Chin Huat Francis v Lim Kok Chye Ivan*[18] gave a strong affirmation of parental responsibility by extending the expectation to two couples who were clearly not the parents of the young girl before the court, but hoping at some point to be appointed her adoptive parents. The Court of Appeal supported its decision not to alter the current living arrangement of the young girl by making observations on what it expects of these two sets of adults.[19] The complete statement from former Chief Justice Yong Pung How deserves to be quoted:

> Both parties have filed adoption [applications]. ... It was the status quo which was clearly beneficial for her overall wellbeing. Little Esther has been subject to too many upheavals, and faced too many emotional trials for an infant of her age. It was our wish to avoid putting any further emotive burdens on her. ... A child is a living being, dependent on adults from birth and must be cherished with genuine love from the outset. ... In any case ... the very least the court must do is to advocate the underlying

premise that parents, natural or potential, must care for their children.[20]

These wise words ought to be periodically repeated to all parents and would-be parents. It is very beneficial for the Women's Charter to have set out the right perspective of the relationship between a child and the adults around him or her, whether they are parents, or persons playing one role or another that parents usually play.

Section 112(1): Giving Equal Credit to Financial and Non-financial Contributions to the Marriage

A provision that is also worthy of close study comes into play only on the termination of marriage by divorce. Section 112(1) empowers the court that grants a judgement which terminates a marital relationship to order the division of their matrimonial assets in "just and equitable" proportions between the soon-to-be former spouses. Life is seamless in the sense that, even upon the termination of marriage, all that ends is the marital relationship. The couple will require the help of the court to reorganize their financial arrangements. If they have young children, there is even more reorganization, including further financial reorganization involved so the post-divorce couple can continue to discharge all their responsibilities. It has rightly been observed that divorce is not an end in itself, but merely a change of form and living arrangements among family members.

The Women's Charter Section 112(1) provides that: "The court shall have power ... to order the division ... of any matrimonial asset ... in such proportions as the court thinks just and equitable." This power bestowed on the divorce court may be the most visible effect of Section 46(1) of the Women's Charter, placing marriage on the moral foundation of being an equal cooperative partnership of different efforts. Section 46(1) may be appreciated to form the basis that propelled the most remarkable development of Singapore's law on the division of matrimonial assets upon divorce.

Modelled on Scandinavian "Deferred Community of Property" Idea via Africa and Malaysia

The provision that is now Section 112(1) was introduced as Section 106 only as recently as the amendment of the Women's Charter in 1980.[21] A review of how it came to be enacted as part of the Women's Charter shows how a good idea can literally travel halfway round the world to find a home here.[22]

The idea of "deferred community of property" brilliantly tweaks the civil law idea of "community of property" (where, upon marriage, all property bought by either party becomes pooled into a community over which both husband and wife have equal right of ownership and control) by deferring this until the termination of a marriage.[23] By so doing, the highly intrusive effect of "community of property" (in giving the spouse of the owner of the property equal rights over the property) does not take hold while their marriage continues. During this time, transactions over property continue as easily as if the owner were not married. It would not be helpful if the law were to be more intrusive into the relationship between husband and wife during the subsistence of their marriage. It has been the experience of other countries that imposing "community of property" during the subsistence of a marriage hampers the smooth transactions regarding the sale and transfer of properties so much so as to hinder the economic process.

Upon the couple's divorce, however, the courts should have one opportunity to look into their property ownership and where, as is common, this is biased heavily in favour of the spouse who assumed the main breadwinner's role, the courts can make an order dividing up their surplus available properties to achieve a just and equitable division between them. The just and equitable division of these properties will, therefore, ensure that both parties, upon divorce, are left with a fair share of the available properties. Both the party who was the main breadwinner, as well as the one who was the main caregiver in the family, will walk away from each other with a fair share of their accummulated wealth and property.

Like all brilliant ideas, "deferred community of property" is simple: it permits the law to facilitate market transactions over a property during the continuance of a marriage, as well as ensure the fair division of the property between the couple upon their divorce. The Scandinavian idea was proposed to be adopted in Malaysia in 1971,[24] apparently in a form modelled after a proposed provision in Kenya.[25]

Thus it was the former Section 106 that was inserted into the Women's Charter in 1980. This former provision was improved on when it was substituted with the current Section 112 in 1996.[26] The Court of Appeal in Singapore twice endorsed this writer's depiction of Section 112 as "deferred community of property" recently.[27]

Division of Matrimonial Assets Assisted by the Moral View of Marriage

This writer has repeatedly related the power of the courts to divide property between divorced former spouses, with Section 46(1) defining their marriage as the equal cooperative partnership of different efforts.[28] The legal view of marriage as a husband and wife's equal cooperative partnership of different efforts for their mutual benefit provides the optimal context for appreciating the court's power to divide their matrimonial assets. No provision other than Section 46(1) can more perfectly justify the "just and equitable" division of matrimonial assets (that is, property that one or other or both spouses acquired by their personal effort during the course of their marriage) upon the termination of the marriage. England still does not have a statutory provision equivalent to the Women's Charter Section 112(1) and English courts struggle from not having the context provided by Section 46(1) within which to exercise their power over the divorced former spouses' property.[29]

The Court of Appeal has adopted this writer's linkage of these two provisions of the Women's Charter with this observation:

> The division of matrimonial assets under the Act is founded on the prevailing ideology of marriage as an equal co-operative partnership of efforts. The contributions of both spouses are equally recognised

whether he or she concentrates on the economics or homemaking role, as both must be performed equally well if the marriage is to flourish. When the marriage breaks up, these contributions are translated into economic assets in the distribution ...[30]

Remarkable Decisions on Division of Matrimonial Assets

The development of the law of division of matrimonial assets in Singapore has been remarkable from its introduction a mere thirty years ago. From the first decision where the courts used this power as it was intended to be used, *Koo Shirley v. Mok Kong Chua Kenneth*, only in 1989,[31] the body of case law has grown dramatically both numerically and substantively. This writer has found that:

> [N]o homemaker wife has been given less than 35% of the matrimonial assets, except in two cases involving 'huge money'. Indeed, homemaker wives who served their roles for 20 years or more have received 50% or even more. The majority of decisions resulted in a simple equal division ordered or an insignificant difference from 50%. ... The next most common proportions were where one spouse received 10% more than the other. With these two categories forming the vast majority of decisions given in recent years, it may be suggested that an order of division of matrimonial assets in Singapore is likely to be of equal division or within a narrow range from equal division.[32]

Instead of unnaturally working out what is the numerical (dollar) value of the housekeeping and caregiving the homemaker wife has performed during the course of a marriage, the approach in Singapore may simply be said to encourage equation of these efforts with the efforts of the breadwinner. It is almost as if half of what the breadwinner earns is attributed to the housekeeping and caregiving provided by the homemaker. This is indeed fairer to the homemaker than if the judges were to attribute a numerical dollar value to housekeeping and caregiving. It avoids the suggestion that the homemaker is no more than an exalted servant and, equally important, it conveys quite correctly to the breadwinner that what the homemaker does at home is equal in value to what the breadwinner does in the public arena.

Lessons from the Singapore Law

The Malaysian Court of Appeal observed in 2003 that while it may be dangerous to rely uncritically on decided cases from other jurisdictions in understanding the Malaysian law on division of matrimonial assets upon divorce, this may not necessarily be so with decisions in Singapore as the two laws share a common origin.[33] The court gave a decision that was consistent with the principles laid down by the High Court in *Koo Shirley v. Mok Kong Chua Kenneth*.[34] The principled basis within Section 46(1) of the Women's Charter has driven the remarkable development of Singapore's law on the division of matrimonial assets so much so that other countries may now draw worthwhile lessons from the judicial record of Singapore. Such is the contribution of the Women's Charter that the law in Singapore may be said to place more or less equal value on the different roles a husband and wife discharge during their marriage.

The law on the division of matrimonial assets may well be one of the finest areas of the law in Singapore. The decisions from its courts stand up to the best in the world. The courts are truly committed to ensuring that all manner of different efforts of a couple, whether they contribute financially to the family coffers, or non-financially to the well-being of the family and care of the children, receive close to equal credit. It is patently clear that all these roles must be performed as well as possible, if the family is to prosper and thrive.

The provision in the Women's Charter Section 112, as much as the provision in Section 46(1), conveys a moral message of what marriage means to the spouses and general society. It is no irony that a moral message can emerge from the part of the Women's Charter that deals with the termination of a marriage. The termination of any marriage is a somewhat unfortunate incident, but a good law acknowledges that this is merely a form of relief that an unhappy couple seeks and that the lives of the family members must go on. Good law helps family members move on, regroup, and aim to thrive again after divorce proceedings are completed. There is every reason for the law to espouse morality even at this transitional phase in their lives.

Conclusion

The Women's Charter of Singapore is a remarkable document, not least for the reasons given above. It contains provisions that allow for the orderly solemnization and recording of a marriage, the basics in legal regulation of the relationships between spouses, and between them and their children, and the regulation of economic matters. Beyond the substance of these provisions that are largely the concern of lawyers, the Women's Charter holds lessons of great utility to the general society in Singapore.

It is the moral messages that one can distil from the Women's Charter that may be even more significant than the legal provisions. It is these messages that guide each of us in how to live our lives with our family members in meaningful and respectful ways. If each person can learn these lessons from the law, Singaporeans will be guided towards the continuity and strengthening of their family relationships. There could be greater efforts made to disseminate information regarding the most significant provisions in the Women's Charter among members of the public in Singapore. If the core provisions can be conveyed in non-legal language to become better known, they will teach all Singaporeans valuable lessons on how to behave as moral members of families. The more people know of what the Women's Charter would like to coax out of each person, the better the whole community of Singaporeans is likely to become.

If we read the law wisely, it serves us beyond its substantive provisions. Significant provisions in the Women's Charter contain useful lessons for lawyers and non-lawyers alike. The Women's Charter was an important tool in the development of Singapore as a nation. It continues to be an important tool in educating and guiding Singaporeans towards living morally respectful lives as members of

families. There is not likely to be another document of law
of equal significance to us.

Notes

1. Cap. 353 of the 1996 Revised Edition of the Statutes of the
   Republic of Singapore.
2. As in Ordinance 18 of Laws of the State of Singapore 1961.
3. The PAP disseminated its election manifesto "The Tasks
   Ahead" as its Five-year Plan for 1959–64 through a series
   of mass rallies (Leong 2008).
4. It appeared that Muslim Singaporeans were not quite as
   dissatisfied with the condition of the marriage and family
   laws that governed their family lives. For discussion of
   the reasons for dissatisfaction among the non-Muslim
   Singaporeans, see Leong (1997), pp. 69–86.
5. See "The Tasks Ahead Part 1", pp. 1 and 4.
6. Announced by Dr Toh Chin Chye, PAP chairman, at a special
   Party Congress on 25 April 1959. See "The Tasks Ahead
   Part 1", pp. 7–8.
7. The reason for this title of what is, in substance, the repository
   of marriage and family law is explained by K.M. Byrne,
   Minister for Labour and Law: "We consider this piece of
   legislation as something outside the ordinary stream of
   legislation ... in the real sense of the word, a Charter for the
   women of our State"; see *Singapore Legislative Assembly
   Debates* 12, no. 1 (6 April 1960): column 485.
8. Its Section 3(2) provides that some of its provisions do not
   apply to Singaporeans who are of the Muslim religion or
   who have married under Muslim law. For a discussion on the
   relationship between non-Muslim and Muslim marriage and
   family laws in Singapore, see Leong (2007), pp. 877–918.
9. For a discussion, see Leong (2007), pp. 877–918.

10. Cap. 3 of the 1999 Revised Edition of Statutes of the Republic of Singapore; see Section 35(2).
11. Cap. 3 of the 1999 Revised Edition of Statutes of the Republic of Singapore; see Section 52(3)(d).
12. Cap. 3 of the 1999 Revised Edition of Statutes of the Republic of Singapore; see Section 52(3)(b) and (c).
13. See Administration of Muslim Law (Amendment) Act 20 of 1999, Supreme Court of Judicature Act, Cap. 322 of the 1999 Revised Edition of the Statutes of the Republic of Singapore, Section 17A; the Supreme Court of Judicature (Transfer of Proceedings Pursuant to Section 17A[2]) Order 2004 (S631/2004); and the Supreme Court of Judicature (Transfer of Proceedings Pursuant to Section 17A[2]) Order 2007 (S673/2007).
14. See *Singapore Legislative Assembly Debates* 12, no. 1 (6 April 1960): column 485. The current Swiss provision is Article 159 of the Swiss Civil Code; see the English translation by the Swiss-American Chamber of Commerce, *Swiss Civil Code I and II* (Zurich: Schulthess Juristische Medien AG, 2007) that says it provides: "The wedding ceremony joins the spouses into a matrimonial union. They mutually undertake to assure the well-being of the union through harmonious co-operation and to jointly care for the children. They shall owe each other fidelity and support."
15. Translation from Huber (1902, p. 143) of *Schweizerisches Civilgesetzbuch, Erlauterungen zum Vorentwurf des Eidgneossischen Justiz -und Polizeidepartements*. For the equivalent significance of the moral view of marriage as a couple's equal cooperative partnership of different efforts in Singapore, see Leong (2002).
16. Cap. 122 of the 1985 Revised Edition of the Statutes of the Republic of Singapore.

17. Cap. 38 of the 2001 Revised Edition of the Statutes of the Republic of Singapore.
18. *Singapore Law Reports (Reissue)* (SLR[R]) 2 (1999): 392.
19. This point has been elaborated in Leong (1999).
20. *Singapore Law Reports (Reissue)* 2 (1999): 392, para. 91.
21. See the Women's Charter (Amendment) Act 26 of 1980.
22. See Leong (1993).
23. See, for example, the Swedish Marriage Code from the 1920s which had a provision on "deferred community of property".
24. See *Report of the Royal Commission on non-Muslim Marriage and Divorce Laws of Malaysia*, 1971.
25. See Crown (1988).
26. For the reasons for substitution, see Leong (2007), pp. 534–36.
27. See Judge of Appeal Andrew Phang in *Lock Yeng Fun v Chua Hock Chye*, SLR(R) 3 (2007): 520, para. 40, and Judge of Appeal V.K. Rajah in *Lau Siew Kim v Yeo Guan Chye Terence*, SLR(R) 2 (2008): 108, para. 81.
28. See Leong (1989); Leong (1996, p. 632); and Leong (2000, p. 208).
29. See Leong (2001) which compares the Women's Charter Section 112, set in the context provided by Section 46(1), favourably with the equivalent law in England that suffers not only from being worded less boldly, but also lacks the setting. This is not to suggest that a bold judiciary cannot make up for these legislative weaknesses. Indeed, a bold House of Lords in their seminal decision in *White v. White* (2001) 1 Appeal Cases 596, reinterpreted their equivalent provision. This brought a comment by English academic Stephen Cretney (2003) that their decision introduced the idea of "community of property" into English law as well.

30. Per Judge of Appeal Andrew Phang Boon Leong in *NK v. NL*, SLR(R) 3 (2007): 743, para. 20.
31. SLR(R) 1 (1989): 244.
32. See Leong (2007), pp. 696–98.
33. See Judge of Court of Appeal Abdul Hamid Mohamed in *Sivanes a/l Rajaratnam v. Usha Rani a/p Subramaniam Malayan Law Journal* 3 (2003): 273.
34. See Leong (2006) following in the spirit of Judge of Court of Appeal Abdul Hamid Mohamed's observation.

References

Cretney, S. "Community of Property Imposed by Judicial Decision". *Law Quarterly Review UK* 119 (2003): 349–52.

Crown, Barry. "Property Division on Dissolution of Marriage". *Malaya Law Review* 30 (1988): 34–61.

Huber, Eugen. *Schweizerisches Civilgesetzbuch, Erlauterungen zum Vorentwurf des Eidgneossischen Justiz -und Polizeidepartements*. Bern, Switzerland: 1902.

Leong Wai Kum. "Fifty Years and More of the Women's Charter of Singapore". *Singapore Journal of Legal Studies* (2008): 1–24.

———. *Elements of Family Law in Singapore*. Singapore: LexisNexis, 2007.

———. "Division of Matrimonial Assets upon Divorce: Lessons from Singapore for Malaysian Practice". In *Developments in Singapore and Malaysian Law*, edited by Alan Tan K.J. and A. Sharom. Singapore: Marshall Cavendish Academic, 2006.

———. "Supporting Marriage Through Description as an Equal Partnership of Efforts". In *International Survey of*

Family Law 2002, edited by A. Bainham. UK: Jordans, 2002.

―――. "The Laws in Singapore and England Affecting Spouses' Property on Divorce". *Singapore Journal of Legal Studies* (2001): 19–52.

―――. "The Just and Equitable Division of Gains Between Equal Former Partners in Marriage". *Singapore Journal of Legal Studies* (2000): 208–40.

―――. "Restatement of the Law of Guardianship and Custody in Singapore". *Singapore Journal of Legal Studies* (1999): 432–93.

―――. *Principles of Family Law in Singapore*. Singapore: Butterworths, 1997.

―――. "Trends and Developments in Family Law". In *Singapore Academy of Law: Review of the Judicial and Legal Reforms in Singapore between 1990 and 1995*, edited by W. Woon. Singapore: Butterworths Asia, 1996.

―――. "Division of Matrimonial Assets: Recent Cases and Thoughts for Reform". *Singapore Journal of Legal Studies* (1993): 351–400.

―――. "Division of Matrimonial Property upon Termination of Marriage". *Malayan Law Journal* 1 (1989): xiii–lvii.

Phang, Andrew. "Lock Yeng Fun v Chua Hock Chye". SLR(R) 3 (2007): 520.

Rajah V.K. "Lau Siew Kim v Yeo Guan Chye Terence". SLR(R) 2 (2008): 108.

Swiss-American Chamber of Commerce. *Swiss Civil Code I and II* (English Translation of the Official Texts). Zurich, Switzerland: Schulthess Juristische Medien AG, 2007.

"The Tasks Ahead Part 1". Singapore: Petir, 1959.

Yong Pung How C.J. "Lim Chin Huat Francis & Anor v Lim Kok Chye Ivan & Anor". SLR(R) 2 (1999): 392.

Legislative Documents

Administration of Muslim Law (Amendment) Act 20 of 1999. Singapore: Government Printers, 1999.

Children and Young Persons Act, Cap. 38, 2001 Revised Edition of the Statutes of the Republic of Singapore. Singapore: Government Printers, 2001.

Guardianship of Infants Act, Cap. 122, 1985 Revised Edition of the Statutes of the Republic of Singapore. Singapore: Government Printers, 1985.

Singapore Legislative Assembly Debates 12, no. 1 (6 April 1960): column 485.

Supreme Court of Judicature Act, Cap. 322, 1999 Revised Edition of the Statutes of the Republic of Singapore, Section 17A. Singapore: Government Printers, 1999.

The Supreme Court of Judicature (Transfer of Proceedings Pursuant to Section 17A[2]) Order 2007 (S673/2007). Singapore: Government Printers, 2007.

———, Order 2004 (S631/2004). Singapore: Government Printers, 2004.

The Women's Charter (Amendment) Act 26 of 1980. Singapore: Government Printers, 1980.

4
A Lawyer's Perspective on How Divorcees View the Women's Charter

Ellen Lee

Introduction

Divorce has increasingly become an inevitable consequence of marriage in many parts of the world. That the incidence of divorce is on the increase worldwide is related to a number of factors. Romantic love — which was commonly thought to dictate the formation of marital unions — is on the demise and has been touted as one reason for the rise in divorce. In this case, once love subsides, divorce is unavoidable (cf. Abbott, Wallace and Tyler 2005). The value placed on individualism, shaping choice, control, and equality is another factor (Beck and Beck-Gernsheim 1995). Other arguments put forward for the increasing rate of divorce include the erosion of the "man as breadwinner" model, owing to cultural changes, and the breaking down of a moral code around marriage, divorce, and cohabitation (Lewis 2001). The erosion of marital commitment owing to dissatisfaction in the relationship has also been found to be a factor leading to divorce, rather than women's economic independence (Sayer and Bianchi 2000).

In almost every country, family laws have incorporated provisions to enable estranged couples to end their unions. In Singapore, the Women's Charter, Chapter 353, is the law that governs divorce of non-Muslims. According to the Women's Charter, "that the marriage has irretrievably broken down", based on any one of the following five "facts" is the sole cause for divorce (Chan 2008):

(a) That the defendant has committed adultery and the plaintiff finds it intolerable to continue living with the defendant;

(b) That the defendant has behaved unreasonably and the plaintiff cannot be reasonably expected to live with the defendant;

(c) That the plaintiff has been deserted for a continuous period of at least two years prior to filing the writ for divorce;

(d) That the parties have lived apart for a continuous period of at least three years immediately before the filing of the writ for divorce and the defendant consents to the divorce been granted; and,

(e) That the parties have lived apart for a continuous period of at least four years immediately before the filing of the writ for divorce.

In a study on divorce in Singapore in the late 1990s, differences in values, ideals, goals, and outlook in life; inability to communicate because of differences in personality or character; and infidelity, were cited as reasons for seeking a divorce (Quah 1999, as cited in Quah 2003).

As in the United States (Braver, Whitley and Ng 1993), a higher proportion of women than men were found to initiate divorce.[1]

Compared with the process in many other countries, filing for a divorce in Singapore is not easy for a number of reasons. That the government places a significant emphasis on the family as the "anchor for individuals and the cornerstone of society"[2] has been cited as a major reason. A pro-family policy is promulgated through the Ministry of Community Development, Youth and Sports (MCYS) which offers a wide range of programmes aimed at encouraging marriage and procreation, championing work-life balance, and helping dysfunctional families. The commitment to promoting the stability of the family is also evidenced in the Family and Juvenile Courts where Family Law judges have the option of referring families to the Counselling and Psychological Services Division (CAPS) within the Subordinate Courts to manage their emotions and resolve their conflicts related to violence, divorce, and children during and after the court process. Project Heart is another programme targeted at couples considering divorce or divorced couples considering reconciliation.[3] In spite of the explicit position taken by the government in matters of family life, divorce continues to be on the rise. In the report "Family First: State of the Family Report 2009", divorce is regarded as a "worrying trend …".[4] Statistics generated by the Singapore Department of Statistics show that divorce is on the rise as the rate of divorce (and annulments) per 1,000 residents was 0.8 in 1980, rising to 1.6 in 2000, and further rising to 2.0 in 2008. As for divorces under the Women's Charter, the total number were 3,924 in 1998 rising to 5,155 in 2008.[5]

In Singapore, couples in troubled marriages have been found often to assume that they would not face obstacles in their quest to end the union. Contrary to popular thinking, a prospective divorcee who wishes to commence divorce proceedings to dissolve his/her marriage, will have to cross several hurdles before the legal proceedings can take effect. When told that the process of divorce is harder than the process of registering a marriage — because of the rights and obligations that accrue upon their exchanging vows to live together until death do them part — most react in disbelief. Because seeking a divorce is a complicated process, some react with anger at having to prove their grounds for the divorce. Since the process is long-drawn, others are angered at having to wait for the court to pronounce the divorce and to approve arrangements regarding the children and division of matrimonial assets. Learning that their needs are not always met by the court further compounds the frustration felt by divorcing couples.

This chapter will highlight the areas of contention related to issues ancillary to the grounds for divorce, ranging from custody, care, control, and access to the child/children and maintenance for them to financial support for the wife; division of the matrimonial assets and the matrimonial home; and whether one party should be ordered to pay the other his/her legal and related costs incurred because of the divorce. In addition, the chapter shows how disputes among couples have emerged, notably in the enforcement of court orders, which have shaped stereotypical perceptions couples hold of the Women's Charter. Oftentimes, divorcing couples harbour grievances because of not receiving what they think is due to them based on the judgements put forward by the court. As a result, divorcing couples who do not receive what they want, or who demand more than what the court has adjudicated as just and equitable, view the Women's Charter as an unfair, unjust, and lopsided piece of legislation.

"Untying the Knot": Jurisdiction and Criteria for Divorce

As mentioned above, for non-Muslims, divorce is regulated by the provisions of the Women's Charter that specifically mandates that legal proceedings commence in the High Court of Singapore. Notwithstanding this, the High Court has transferred its jurisdiction to hear these cases to the Family Court. The divorce of Muslims, in contrast, is governed by the provisions of the Administration of Muslim Law Act, Chapter 3, which has its own Syariah Court to hear and rule on marital disputes. But on issues of maintenance, whether in respect of an application for an order for the husband to pay maintenance, or the enforcement of maintenance orders granted to the wife or ex-wife or the child/children of the marriage, or an application for Personal Protection Orders (PPOs) to prevent family violence, Muslims, like non-Muslims, can initiate proceedings or enforce their claims in the Family Court (see Chapter 3 in this volume). This dichotomy of court systems, however, creates confusion for the applicant who is not represented by a lawyer. In addition, Muslim applicants have been found "to run to two Courts", depending on what kind of relief is being sought. For example, a Muslim woman has to go to the

Syariah Court to dissolve her marriage and obtain judgement for the ancillary issues. If she encounters family violence from her husband while the divorce proceedings are in progress, or her husband fails to pay interim maintenance for her and/or her child/children, she will have to go to the Family Court to seek help.

Part X, Chapter 1 of the Women's Charter deals with divorce and related matters. Before commencing a divorce, the plaintiff must satisfy either the nationality or residential requirement. Section 93 requires one of the parties to be domiciled in Singapore or to have been habitually residing in Singapore for at least three years immediately before filing for divorce (see Chan 1996). This is usually interpreted to mean that one of the parties has to be a Singapore citizen. If neither party is a citizen, then one of them must be a Singapore permanent resident or, if not granted permanent residency yet, he/she must have been residing in Singapore for at least three consecutive years prior to commencing divorce proceedings.

Married expatriates who come from countries where divorce laws do not insist on satisfying domicile or residential requirements are baffled by the Women's Charter's stringent requirements. Foreign brides or grooms, who for some reason want to get out of their marriage with spouses who also do not satisfy this requirement, tend to view the Women's Charter as being too restrictive in this regard. Couples who are adamant about divorcing but are unable to satisfy this basic requirement, have been known to leave Singapore to file for their divorce in their country of origin instead, especially if the divorce laws there are comparatively less stringent.

The Women's Charter also disallows couples from filing a writ for divorce within the first three years of the marriage in accordance to Section 94(1). The rationale for this restriction is to give newlyweds time to adjust to married life and resolve their differences before rushing headlong into divorce. While the restriction is meant to send the message that the institution of marriage should be taken seriously, some have argued that a three-year restriction could be reduced to a year and that it would have the same effect since the "restriction alone cannot achieve the goal of stabilizing marriages ..." (Ong 2003, p. 431).

Putting these arguments aside, one should note that this restriction has had a negative impact on the "afflicted party", especially for victims of physical violence. From the perspective of such victims, the law should not unreasonably tie them down to an abusive spouse and force them to live out the three-year period. For couples who discover incompatibilities with each other shortly after marriage and want out, the waiting time cannot be shortened either even if both parties agree to end the union. In such a case, the parties usually feel that this requirement is unjust, and that they are entitled to end the marriage for having married the "wrong" spouse in the first place.

Fortunately, the Women's Charter provides an "escape clause" in Section 94(2). If the plaintiff satisfies the court by demonstrating that the marriage is one of exceptional hardship suffered by him/her, or of exceptional depravity on the part of the defendant, the court may not insist on strict compliance with the three-year period. In such cases, the applicant takes out a pre-divorce application to prove the exceptional hardship or the exceptional depravity. It is only when the court is satisfied with the evidence that the applicant would be granted leave to file the writ and proceed with the divorce. However, that which constitutes "exceptional hardship" and "exceptional depravity" are not defined in the Women's Charter; instead these terms are interpreted largely on the facts of each case. Successful applications are those in which the plaintiff is able to prove that the defendant has used excessive family violence that caused the plaintiff to suffer psychological, emotional, or physical trauma and irreparable harm.

Nonetheless, it is the plaintiff who feels the greatest injustice because he/she is forced to resort to two sets of legal proceedings: one to prove the exceptional hardship he/she has suffered, or exceptional depravity on the part of the defendant which would qualify him/her to file for the divorce within the first three years of marriage, and the other, which refers to the actual filing of the divorce proper in order to end the marriage. Emotions tend to run high in this situation because of the higher legal costs incurred and the excessive time taken to settle the divorce.

Adultery and Unreasonable Behaviour: Two "Facts" of Divorce

The Women's Charter recognizes adultery to be a fact for divorce. In order to prove adultery, the plaintiff has to produce direct evidence that the defendant had sexual intercourse with a third party who could be sued as a co-defendant if the third party's identity is ascertained. This type of evidence, however, is often hard to come by unless the defendant is already living with the third party; the defendant and the third party have a child out of wedlock; or the defendant and the third party are found to have had a sexual relationship. In this last instance, a photograph of the defendant with the third party alone or in intimate moments such as kissing, hugging, or holding hands, are not enough to satisfy the requirement of the law to prove adultery. Letters or cards written in romantic tones are not regarded as evidence, just as condoms found in the defendant's possession are not either.

Owing to the requirement of direct evidence, the plaintiff will have to hire a private investigator to trail the defendant in order to produce proof of adultery to the court. Proof here is based on the private investigator's surveillance report that, given the time and circumstances, there was opportunity and probability that sexual intercourse could have taken place, for example, in a hotel room or an apartment where the defendant and the third party have spent sufficient time together for the illicit union to have taken place.

But the evidence for adultery becomes weak if the plaintiff continues to live with the defendant. Section 95(5)(b) states that if, after the plaintiff's discovery of the defendant's adultery, the plaintiff continues to live with the defendant for a period exceeding six months, then the plaintiff's justification for divorce based on adultery is no longer valid. In addition, the plaintiff's claim that it is intolerable to live with the defendant would be ruled out. This would mean that the plaintiff is forced to rely on the private investigator's report, if it shows that the adultery took place less than six months before the writ for divorce is filed.

Mustering evidence for adultery on the part of the defendant may be difficult or near impossible for the plaintiff for other reasons. For many, making use of the services of a private investigator may not be an option for two reasons. First, it is seen as too onerous, especially when the cost of hiring a private investigator is usually very high. Second, that the report is valid for only six months has been viewed by many to be too arbitrary. There have been instances when the potential plaintiff suspects the potential defendant of infidelity and proceeds to obtain confirmation of the potential defendant's actions. Yet when confronted with proof of the adultery, the potential plaintiff is too devastated to react calmly or think clearly. In this case, the potential plaintiff has been found not to seek legal advice and, as a result, is unaware of the six-month requirement under Section 95(5)(b) of the Women's Charter. Time is lost as the six-month period slips by and the fact of adultery cannot be relied upon even when there is the private investigator's report to produce as proof. While to the potential plaintiff, the proof is cast in stone and that he/she should have been allowed to rely on the private investigator's report indefinitely, the law says otherwise.

Just like the wives in such cases, husbands too harbour the belief that when they rely on adultery as proof of the irretrievable breakdown of the marriage, they are in a stronger bargaining position to claim custody, care, and control of the children, and deny their wives access to them. Husbands also erroneously think that they need not pay maintenance to the adulterous wives. Conversely, wives think that adulterous husbands would have to pay maintenance to them and their children and that they would get a larger share of the matrimonial assets. Both the wife and the husband share the misconception that hefty legal and related costs, including reimbursement of the private investigator's costs, would have to be paid by the guilty party. In reality, their assumptions are wrong, especially since adultery merely gives the aggrieved party the right to end the marriage, but not to make related demands on the settlement of the divorce.

"Unreasonable behaviour" is another fact for divorce. As in adultery, it is difficult to prove the acts considered to be unreasonable behaviour as these are, more often than not, acts or behaviour for which there is no proof or witness. In order to satisfy Section 95(6) of the Women's Charter, the plaintiff has to ensure that he/she does not live with the defendant for a period of more than six months after the final incident relied on to substantiate his/her claim that he/she cannot reasonably be expected to live with the defendant.

"Separation": Another "Fact" for Divorce

Living separately for a stipulated period is also a fact for divorce according to the law in Singapore. Of the five factors on which divorce proceedings' may be started, living separately and apart from the other party is usually the hardest to comprehend for the ordinary person. This occurs especially when the couple no longer has a conjugal relationship with each other and live in separate rooms, although they may live under the same roof for many years. For the wife who cooks, washes, irons, and cleans for the family, she may continue to do so out of a sense of obligation, especially when her husband continues to provide financially for her because she manages the household. While she is clearly only "performing her duty", she has no more romantic feelings towards her husband. Being sensitive to her children's needs in her nurturer role, she may end up going out with her husband and children on family outings for the sake of the children. Unfortunately under the Women's Charter, the plaintiff who goes about the daily activities of her life, as if there were no problems in the marriage, does not satisfy the requirement of "living separately and apart from each other", as the intention to end the marriage has not been clearly manifested in her actions. What is required is that the couple intending to divorce must not be seen as a family by a third party.

But the court is not uniformly rigid in this "fact" when deciding a divorce. Because neither party can buy or rent another Housing Development Board (HDB) flat before the marriage is dissolved by the court, therefore the plaintiff is often forced to live with the defendant and, in most instances, the two sleep in separate bedrooms after one of them has formed the intention to end the conjugal relationship. This arrangement is usually regarded as "living separately and apart from each other", provided they lead their lives as complete strangers and do not eat, sleep, or go out together as a family with their children, to satisfy the requisite three or four years, as laid down in Section 95(3)(d) or (e) of the Women's Charter.

Living apart for at least three years is a necessary condition in this "fact" for divorce. The difference between using three years or four years of separation as evidence to prove the "irretrievable breakdown of the marriage" is that the plaintiff has to produce the defendant's written consent, if the parties' have lived apart for only three years. This requirement does not apply if they have lived apart for four years. Hence, if the plaintiff wants to avoid a contested divorce, he/she will have a stronger case if he/she lives apart from the spouse for four years before filing for divorce so the defendant cannot challenge the facts of the divorce. Contrast this with using two years of continuous living apart from each other under the fact of "desertion" provided for under Section 95(3)(c) of the Women's Charter. This will be relatively simpler. All that the plaintiff needs to prove is the fact of the defendant having abandoned the plaintiff for a continuous period of at least two years immediately preceding the filing of the writ. But if there was any period during which the parties resumed living together for six months or more during the two, three or four years, then the period during which they had been living separately will not count towards the period of desertion or separation to be cited for the divorce.

From the above, it is clear that the Women's Charter does place the plaintiff in the unenviable position of having to satisfy a number of requirements before he/she is able to file for divorce. It is not surprising, therefore, that plaintiffs often regard such obligations as being unduly onerous and not in their favour, especially when they see themselves as victims of a marriage gone sour through no fault of theirs. Hence, it is difficult for them to see the Women's Charter as offering them any protection at all since they have to fulfil such stringent requirements before they even reach the doorsteps of the Family Court.

The Divorce Process: Serving the Writ and Related Documents

On taking action to dissolve the marriage, the plaintiff must also ensure that he/she complies with the rules that regulate the divorce process. Here, the law contained in the Women's Charter has to be read together with the rules contained in the Matrimonial Proceedings Rules (MPR) which are the subsidiary legislation governing the procedural processes applicable to all divorces. The MPR, including certain provisions contained in the Rules of Court, another set of subsidiary legislation that prescribes the mode and forms to be used in all civil court claims, also apply in all divorce proceedings.

Under Rule 11 of the MPR, the writ of divorce and all related documents must be sent to the defendant and co-defendant either personally or by registered post, as in the case of adultery where the identity of the co-defendant is known and the plaintiff wishes to include the co-defendant as a party to the proceedings. The plaintiff's lawyer knows the actions to be taken even if the defendant or co-defendant takes steps to avoid being served with the documents to frustrate the legal proceedings. When the plaintiff, however, does not appoint a lawyer to represent him/her in the divorce, he/she may stand the risk of not complying with Rule 11 and, therefore, may not satisfy the court that he/she has complied with the MPR to bring the fact of the divorce to the attention of the defendant and/or the co-defendant so as to allow the defendant and/or the co-defendant an opportunity to defend themselves.

Whether the defendant resides in Singapore, at the time the plaintiff initiates divorce proceedings, will determine if these can be carried out. If the defendant does not reside in Singapore at the time the writ has to be served on him/her, then the plaintiff must comply strictly with Rule 12 and the Rules of Court that legislate how the divorce documents should be brought to the attention of the defendant before the plaintiff can proceed further with the divorce. Proof of service is important as it means that the defendant and/or the co-defendant is/are aware of the proceedings stated against them, and that they are given an opportunity to rebut the allegations made by the plaintiff. Moreover, the defendant and/or the co-defendant must file a prescribed document known as the "Memorandum of Appearance" to inform the court and the plaintiff of their response to the plaintiff's case and claims, within the time given by the Registrar of the Family Court, if the divorce documents have been successfully brought to their attention. If the defendant is based in Singapore, he/she has eight days after receipt of the divorce documents to submit the "Memorandum of Appearance" to inform the court and the plaintiff of his/her decision regarding the divorce. If the defendant is not based or present in Singapore, it is usual to grant this party thirty days to submit the "Memorandum of Appearance".

It is common to find that the plaintiff is not able to understand the rationale for the Women's Charter not entrusting him/her with the onus of informing the defendant of the commencement of the divorce, especially if the plaintiff and defendant are still living under the same roof. From the plaintiff's perspective, he/she sees his/her active role at this stage to be a way of making sure the defendant does not try to dodge service of the divorce documents once the plaintiff's lawyers have set the divorce proceedings in motion. The plaintiff may also conclude that the court should be cognizant of the fact that the defendant or co-defendant already knows that the plaintiff has started divorce proceedings, instead of saddling the plaintiff with a series of compliance rules which he/she perceives as working in favour of the defendant or co-defendant by giving them more time and opportunity to challenge the plaintiff's claim and to file their counterclaim. Fear on the part of the plaintiff is real especially since the counterclaim can make the divorce more expensive in the long run. Thus, it is not uncommon for parties to be worn out by contentious divorce proceedings marked by "Counterclaims", the "Defence to Counterclaim", and the "Reply to Defence to Counterclaim". As a result, what some couples may assume to be a simple divorce procedure may well turn out to be a very complicated process, lasting much longer than they had originally thought.

"Settling the Divorce": Custody, Care and Control, and Other Matters

Clearly, it takes time for a divorce to be settled. The court will have to be satisfied that the plaintiff has proven his/her case before it grants an interim judgement for divorce, usually with the pronouncement that it will be made final in three months. At the same time, the court will give an order on ancillary matters: custody, care and control and access of the children of the marriage; the children's maintenance; maintenance for the wife either to be paid periodically or in a lump sum; the division of the matrimonial home and of matrimonial assets; and costs to be awarded to the plaintiff or the defendant, if there is a counterclaim. If, however, the parties cannot settle the ancillary matters on their own, the court may advise mediation as a preliminary step for them to reach some kind of compromise. If this fails, the parties may proceed to trial. The preliminary step is to save them substantial legal costs and time which they will have to incur if each party has to prove or deny every allegation raised by the other. Following the exchange of the respective documents each is intending to use to prove their claims, the court may direct the parties to file an Affidavit of Assets and Means. The hearing of ancillary matters is presided by a judge who hears the arguments put forward by the parties' respective lawyers without the plaintiff or the defendant being present. These arguments are usually based on the facts and evidence set out in the plaintiff's and defendant's affidavits, which are statements made on oaths. The parties' respective affidavits will set out his/her income, assets and liabilities, the extent of contributions each party has made to the acquisition and preservation of the matrimonial home or assets, and the basis on which the parties are staking their claims.

Custody, Care and Control, and Access to Children

In a divorce situation, the court has the power to grant one of the parents the responsibility to raise the child/children in accordance with Section 126 of the Women's Charter. "Custody" is not defined in the Women's Charter, but is generally regarded as having the decision-making power over three important aspects of the child's/children's life, such as which school the child/children should attend, which religion the child/children should embrace, and what medical care the child/children ought to receive if the need arises. "Care and control" refers to other day-to-day matters concerning the child's/children's living arrangement, upbringing, and well-being that will be the responsibility of one parent. The parent who does not have care and control will have access rights to the child/children. If the divorcing couple can agree on the child's/children's living arrangement, the court need not adjudicate on the matter (Ong 2007). But if the couple is unable to agree on whom the child/children should live with, the court steps in to make an order of care and control.

There are different ways in which custody, care and control, and access may be decided by the court. It may decide to award one parent care and control and the other parent access rights while making no orders concerning custody. In this arrangement, the parent with care and control has the responsibility of managing the day-to-day affairs of the child while the other parent is granted contact time with the child by the court. In such a case, because no order of "custody" is made, both parents continue to be involved in the three major aspects of the child's life and retain the right to make decisions in the best interest of the child. It is also possible for the court to make an order of joint custody, which is an explicit way of saying that both parents shall continue to retain their parental rights over the child's life, and the parent who has care and control should consult the parent who only has access to the child. In contrast to this is an order for sole custody. Here, only one parent makes all the decisions while the other parent has no role at all in the child's upbringing. It used to be that the parent — more often than not the mother — who has care and control, is also granted sole custody, while the other parent, usually the father, is left with access to the child but has no involvement in all other matters related to the child's development. The court has since become more inclined to changing this trend, recognizing that it is the child's/children's rights to have both parents make decisions for him/her/them. The assumption here is that the child/children should be entitled to have both parents consult each other in order to make decisions beneficial to him/her/them. In this case, the court expects the divorcing parents to put aside their acrimony towards each other when it comes to important matters concerning their child/children. Because of this, the court now gives joint custody orders in almost all cases, unless there are exceptional grounds, such as, if both parents are living in different countries after the divorce, which makes the joint decision process cumbersome or difficult. Or if one of the parents has been proven to have been abusive towards the child/children, then it is in the child's/children's paramount interest and welfare that the abusive parent is not granted custody at all.

There is a common perception that the Women's Charter is pro-woman and pro-mother and against men as fathers or husbands. In other words, the Women's Charter is perceived to be gender-biased in that it protects women's interests only. This has left both men and women to conclude that in matters of claims of custody, care and control of the children who are under twenty-one years old, the court will rule in favour of women. Although the law may support mothers to a greater degree as it recognizes that the maternal relationship is the primary bond between parent and child, in cases where the father can prove his effort and sincerity in bonding with the child, the court may decide on care and control to his advantage instead. Working mothers, in particular, risk losing care and control of their children, especially if they have slackened by prioritizing their role in wage work over care work (Ong 2007). Thus, while the court acknowledges the mother as the primary caregiver, it is simultaneously aware of not "over-playing this aspect ... in favour of a mother solely on the basis of her maternal position" (Ong 2007, p. 90).

There are other perceptions (and misconceptions as well) of the Women's Charter — usually consisting of stereotypical expectations of how the Charter benefits either party based on their gender identity. For example, it is common to see mothers expecting to be granted custody, care and control of daughters, while their husbands would be granted custody, care and control of sons. This is commonly referred to as "split" custody. Another instance of split custody is when mothers expect to be given the custody, care and control of infants as well as younger children, on the assumption that the child is at his/her stage of life where he/she is unable to take care of his/her immediate needs by himself/herself. Another misleading assumption is that mothers who have not worked during the marriage, or who have stopped working or are unemployed at the time of the divorce, would not be granted custody, care and control since they would not be able to support themselves and their children. Therefore, when the court does not rule in favour of the wife in the way she thinks it should, or when the husband's expectations are not met, both husband and wife may end up unanimously accusing the Women's Charter of not protecting women, from the wife's perspective, and of being biased against men, from the husband's perspective.

Although the court's decision relating to custody, care and control of children is definitive, it is not unheard of that the parent granted care and control of the children restricts the other parent's access to the children. The most common reasons put forward are: the children are fearful of their fathers; the husbands have neglected the children and have not been taking care of them since they were young and, hence, do not know what the children need; the fathers do not have the capacity to tend to the children's needs; or as fathers, they would not be able to tend to the needs of their daughters who have reached puberty. There are also parents who strongly feel that only they know what is best for their children. Often, it is these parents who are resentful of being told what to do by counsellors, social workers, mediators, and even the judge.

Maintenance for Children

Divorce always has repercussions on children of the estranged couple. Section 46(1) of the Women's Charter provides that upon the solemnization of their marriage, both husband and wife should be mutually bound to cooperate with each other in safeguarding the interests of the union and in caring and providing for the children, although this injunction is not restricted to monetary contributions only.

Section 68 states very clearly that it is the duty of parents to maintain their children except if the court orders otherwise. Maintenance includes accommodation, clothing, food, and education commensurate to the defendant's means and station in life. Even for divorcing couples, the law explicitly maintains that they continue to uphold these responsibilities and duties towards their children regardless of the dissolution of the marriage. It is only when the child reaches twenty-one years of age, or if he/she should be gainfully employed before then, that the maintenance order ceases (Chan 1996). However there are exceptions to this rule, particularly among children with physical or mental disability (Leong 1979).

But this requirement has not gone down well with husbands. Husbands have regarded this provision as being weighted against them, especially if they have been denied access to their children by their wives or former wives whether during the marriage, during the divorce proceedings, or after the divorce. They become indignant about the Women's Charter protecting errant wives who deliberately and unreasonably withhold their access to their children. A common line of thought on their part is to ask: "Why should we be made to pay for the upkeep of our children if our wives deliberately want to cut off our children's ties with their natural fathers and yet expect us fathers to continue to provide for them?" Their anger is particularly intense in post-divorce situations where enforcement of maintenance orders is sought by their ex-wives.

This duty of providing maintenance remains whether the children are left in the defendant's custody or the custody of a guardian. In this case, the Women's Charter has gone further to provide in Section 70(1) that where a person has accepted a child who is not his child as a member of his family, it will be his duty to provide maintenance for the child (see also Leong 1979). The person is expected to take on this responsibility so long as the father or mother of the child fails to do so, and the court has made such orders to ensure the welfare of the child.

For husbands who marry divorced women with care and control of children from a previous marriage, this duty may be onerous for them. Some may be willing to assume full responsibility for supporting these children only in the case where the children are obedient or respectful towards them. There are instances in which the children whom they are supporting are not obedient and respectful towards them and, in such cases, it is not uncommon for the husbands to feel the injustice or unfairness of having to support these children. This is especially the case where the latter do not regard them as their stepfathers and, consequently, do not demonstrate care towards them, or worse, react negatively to them and treat them with disdain.

The duty to maintain illegitimate children has given rise to some consternation among wives as well. Among them, their fear is that this law may allow illegitimate children to inherit the husband's estate and, therefore, compete with their own legitimate children.

Maintenance for the Wife

Like divorce laws in other countries, the Women's Charter ensures that a divorced wife will receive maintenance which is "awarded on the basis of need, on the principle of financial preservation" (Chan 1996, p. 574). Section 113 empowers the court to order a man to pay maintenance to his wife or former wife at different stages of the matrimony:

(a) during the course of any matrimonial proceedings, for instance, when the wife is applying for a PPO to restrain the husband from committing family violence against her and/or her child/children, or when she is applying for an interim order for custody, care and control of the child/children during any period of separation of the parties, but before divorce proceedings have started; or

(b) when granting, or subsequent to the granting of a judgement of divorce. This means, it is still the responsibility of the husband to continue to support the wife before the divorce proceedings are concluded, and also after the court has granted a divorce based on one of the five facts of irretrievable breakdown of the marriage, but before the settlement of the ancillary matters is reached.

As in maintenance for children, the maintenance order for the wife may cease to apply on two conditions: if not secured, it terminates on the death of either party and, if secured, it terminates on the death of the wife. Also, the man is no longer mandated by law to maintain his former wife if she remarries (Leong 2007; see also Chan 1996). The assumption here is that her new husband, in the case of a woman who remarries, will become her provider.

On the matter of the maintenance order, other misconceptions also exist. Both women and men often mistakenly think that as long as the wife is gainfully employed, she is not allowed to claim maintenance for herself. This assumption is unfounded, however, as shown in the provisions of Sections 69 and 113. The Women's Charter provides in Section 69(4) that the court, when ordering maintenance for a wife, should consider all the circumstances of the case including the following matters:

(a) the financial needs of the wife;
(b) the income, earning capacity (if any), property, and other financial resources of the wife;
(c) any physical or mental disability of the wife;
(d) the age of each party in the marriage and the duration of the marriage;
(e) the contributions made by each party to the welfare of the family, including any contribution made by looking after the home or caring for the family;
(f) the standard of living enjoyed by the wife before the husband neglected or refused to provide reasonable maintenance for the wife; and
(g) the conduct of each party to the marriage, if the conduct is such that it would, in the opinion of the court, be inequitable to disregard it.

From this section, it is clear that the law does not discriminate against working women in claims made for a maintenance order.

Both husbands and wives seeking a divorce have been found to have their own share of grouses on the provisions of Section 69. Most well-to-do husbands are averse to Section 69(4)(f) as it is seen as a licence for wives to claim astronomical sums for themselves by exaggerating their living standards during the marriage. Wives are also disappointed that despite this subsection, the court does not always protect them in this respect, especially when husbands claim that they lack the economic means to continue to provide them with the same lifestyle to which they have been accustomed.

If the divorce proceedings have been started against the husband's wishes by a wife who is adamant in wanting to end the marriage because of his adultery, unreasonable behaviour, desertion, or the parties' separation, he is more likely to feel that the Women's Charter does not protect him. In spite of having committed any of these matrimonial faults, it is likely that he feels that he had not caused the irretrievable breakdown of the marriage and did not file for divorce from the woman whom he still regards as his lawfully wedded wife.

The feeling of injustice is even greater and the reluctance to pay maintenance to the wife is even more pronounced if it is the wife who is guilty of adultery, unreasonable behaviour, deserting him, or initiating the separation. Obviously, the power of the court in Section 71(1) to enforce the maintenance order through the imprisonment of the errant husband — who has the means to pay, but deliberately disobeys the court order — of one month for every month's maintenance not paid, does not go down well with husbands who default on their payment obligation; neither does the making of a garnishee order of the unpaid maintenance on any income, assets, or payments due to the husband, or an attachment of earnings order to secure the maintenance payments through the husband's employers under Section

81(1) (Chan 1996). Some, in particular, take exception to the fact that a sentence of imprisonment does not affect or diminish the husband's obligation to make the payments ordered by the court. However, it is entirely at the court's discretion, if it thinks fit, to reduce the amount of such payments. The sentence of imprisonment is to reflect the court's displeasure with the husband for being in contempt of court by disobeying the maintenance order made against him. The time he has to serve in prison is not intended to be in lieu of making payments of the maintenance, or be regarded as a substitute for the payment of maintenance, unlike in criminal matters where the court has the power to order convicted persons to pay a fine, or to serve time in prison equivalent to the sum they have to pay, if they cannot pay the penalty imposed by the court.

Division of Matrimonial Assets

When granting the divorce, the court is empowered by Section 112 of the Women's Charter to make an order to divide the matrimonial assets between the ex-couple in specific proportions the court considers just and equitable, after seeing proof of the contributions made by each spouse to support his/her claim. It can also order the matrimonial assets to be sold and the sale proceeds to be divided between the ex-couple in such proportions that the court sees as just and equitable. This would include the division of the flat or house that the parties have lived in during the marriage and all other assets whether held in one or both parties' names. In making the decision to divide the matrimonial assets, the court will take into account whether the assets were accumulated through the efforts of one or both parties. In the case where both parties were involved in the acquisition of assets, the court is inclined towards dividing the assets equally between the divorcing couple. But if one party has put in more effort than the other, the court does not necessarily decide on a greater share in favour of that party. An example may be that of a spouse who does not have his/her name registered in the matrimonial home or assets because he/she did not contribute to the purchase of the property and, therefore, was excluded from its ownership. Or the spouse could be a foreigner or a bankrupt at the time of the property acquisition and was, thus, disqualified from its ownership. Moreover, the marriage could have lasted several years during which the non-financially contributing spouse played a critical role in serving the welfare of the family, having sacrificed his/her career, particularly to undertake homemaking tasks and providing care to children or other family members, such as parents or parents-in-laws or siblings-in-law who needed care and supervision, as in the case of elderly, ill or disabled persons. In this case, "the intent of the legislature is to benefit the homemaker-spouse, which should result in a more equal division ..." (Chan 1996, p. 580). But there are exceptions, for example, if the marriage lasted only for a short duration, or if one party did not adequately fulfil his/her breadwinning or homemaking role.

Although this section of the Women's Charter is generally considered to be fair and laudable, not all parties are necessarily happy with the decision of the court. What is often problematic is the expectation of how much would be considered "just and equitable". To try and ensure that all parties are satisfied with such an order, the court would have to scrutinize all the circumstances of the case, including the factors set out in Section 112(2) of the Women's Charter.

The sharpest criticism directed at this particular section of the Women's Charter comes from men. It is not difficult to understand why men have attacked the Women's Charter for favouring women since it is the men who are forced to share their assets with their wives, although they may have been the more active contributor to the matrimonial assets. It is interesting to note that some wives, who might otherwise not have been able to have a share of the husbands' assets for themselves if not for the provisions laid out in the Women's Charter, have also denounced the Charter for not protecting their interests, especially if the division of matrimonial assets ultimately adjudicated by the court falls short of their expectations.

The Case of Family Violence

Although family violence is not laid down explicitly as a fact for divorce, it is used as one of the examples of a spouse's unreasonable behaviour (see also Chapter 5 in this volume). It is further used as a reason to block access to children by divorcees granted a PPO to restrain the person against whom the PPO is made from using family violence against the victim. Some wives or ex-wives also request expedited orders to be issued when applying for their PPOs. They then abuse the expedited orders granted to them to prevent their husbands or ex-husbands from having access to their children before the summons is heard. This is easily done by exaggerating the extent of the family violence allegedly committed by the husband or ex-husband, and claiming that the family violence will be repeated or that there is imminent danger of family violence being committed, unless the court restrains it by issuing the expedited order in the interim before the summons hearing.

It is also quite common for a husband to make a cross-application for a PPO for himself or his child/children as a strategy to force his wife to withdraw her application. The current court system, however, does not allow the "flushing out" of such frivolous applications or abuses until the trial takes place and the court then determines whether to grant the PPO based on the evidence produced during the trial that would warrant the issuance of the order. Even if the court finds that the application is not supported by the evidence produced or testimony given by the complainant, or that the complainant's case has been effectively rebutted by the respondent during the trial, the court has no power to impose a penalty for the frivolous or unproven claim. The court can only admonish the complainant for wasting the time of both the court and the respondent, by having them respond to the summons and, consequently, order the complainant to pay the respondent the costs of the proceedings for his/her actions. Thus, the case is simply dismissed where no protection order is made. In the interim, a respondent who is genuinely victimized by vicious family members has no recourse to prevent the abuse from continuing, and is instead forced to wait at least a few months before the hearing takes place.

Personal Protection Orders that are granted during the marriage remain valid and can survive the dissolution of the marriage. Husbands who have PPOs made against them thus regard these terms as unfair, as they feel that the PPOs should also come to an end after the divorce is finalized and the marriage is dissolved. That the PPOs still have effect after the divorce has been regarded as an anomaly as well, because former spouses have been found to rely on the PPO to obstruct their ex-spouses' access to children. It is also not uncommon for wives to use the PPO as a justification to exert pressure or place demands on their husbands during the ancillary matters stage, by asking for sole custody, care and control of their child/children, or restricting the husbands' access to the child/children, or asking for higher maintenance sums for themselves or their child/children, or even for a larger share of the matrimonial assets or the matrimonial home.

Conclusion

When the Women's Charter was promulgated, it was hailed as a progressive piece of legislation that outlaws polygamy and protects the rights, interests, and welfare of married couples and their children. Over the years, several amendments have been made because of changing times and circumstances as the needs of the populace change (Chan 1996; Leong 1979). The last major amendment was made in 1996. At that time, there was also a call for the Women's Charter to be renamed the "Family Charter" or the "Marriage Charter", amongst other titles, as recommended earlier on

(Leong 1979; see Chapter 3 in this volume), but this plea has not been accepted by the legislature.

Irrespective of what the Women's Charter is called, it is the spirit and intent of this piece of legislation that are more important. While it may not be universally well received by both married men and women seeking divorce, as the discussion above has shown, by and large it has been instrumental in protecting the rights of both men and women. This by no means suggests that this legislation is without flaws and need not undergo amendments in the future. In view of the changing roles of couples and the different responsibilities that each has to assume in the family, there will always be a need to review the Women's Charter periodically to make it relevant to the times.

Notes

1. See <http://www.singstat.gov.sg/stats/themes/people/marriages.pdf> (accessed 20 July 2009).
2. See <http://www.nfc.org.sg/pdf/NFC-StateoftheFamily Report.pdf> (accessed 30 July 2009).
3. See <http://app.subcourts.gov.sg/family/page.aspx? pageid=3758> (accessed 31 July 2009).
4. See <http://www.nfc.org.sg/pdf/NFC-StateoftheFamily Report.pdf> (accessed 30 July 2009).
5. See <http://www.singstat.gov.sg/pubn/popn/smd2008.pdf> (accessed 20 April 2010).

References

Abbott, Pamela, Claire Wallace, and Melissa Tyler. *An Introduction to Sociology: Feminist Perspectives*. 3rd. ed. London: Routledge, 2005.

Beck, Ulrich and Elisabeth Beck-Gernsheim. *The Normal Chaos of Love*. Cambridge, UK: Polity Press, 1995.

Braver, Sanford L., Marnie Whitley, and Christine Ng. "Who Divorced Whom? Methodological and Theoretical Issues". *Journal of Divorce and Remarriage* 20 (1993): 1–19.

Chan Wing Cheong. "Trends in Non-Muslim Divorces in Singapore". *International Journal of Law, Policy and the Family* 22, no. 91 (2008): 91–121.

———. "Latest Improvements to the Women's Charter". *Singapore Journal of Legal Studies* (1996): 553–59.

"Family First: State of the Family Report 2009". Singapore: The National Family Council and the Ministry of Community Development, Youth and Sports, 2009. <http://www.nfc.org.sg/pdf/NFC-StateoftheFamilyReport.pdf> (accessed 30 July 2009).

"Key Indicators on Marriages and Divorces, 2004–2009". *Statistics on Marriages & Divorces 2009*, p. ix. <http://www.singstat.gov.sg/stats/themes/people/marriages.pdf> (accessed 20 July 2009).

Leong Wai Kum. *Elements of Family Law in Singapore*. Singapore: LexisNexis, 2007.

———. "A Turning Point in Singapore Family: Women's Charter (Amendment) Bill 1979". *Malaya Law Review* 21 (1979): 327–51.

Lewis, Jane. *The End of Marriage? Individualism and Intimate Relations*. Cheltenham, UK: Edward Elgar Publishing, 2001.

Ong, Debbie. "The Career Mother in Matrimonial and Custody Proceedings in Singapore". In *Working and Mothering in Asia: Images, Ideologies and Identities*, edited by T.W. Devasahayam and B.S.A. Yeoh. Singapore and Denmark: National University of Singapore Press and Nordic Institute of Asian Studies, 2007.

————. "Time Restriction on Divorce in Singapore". *Singapore Journal of Legal Studies* (2003): 418–43.

"Project HEART". <http://app.subcourts.gov.sg/family/page. aspx?pageid=3758> (accessed 31 July 2009).

Quah, Stella R. *Home and Kin: Families in Asia*. Singapore: Eastern Universities Press, 2003.

Sayer, Liana C. and Suzanne M. Bianchi. "Women's Economic Independence and the Probability of Divorce: A Review and Reexamination". *Journal of Family Issues* 21, no. 7 (2000): 906–43.

"Statistics on Marriages & Divorces 2008". Singapore: Department of Statistics, Ministry of Trade and Industry, 2008. <http:// www.singstat.gov.sg/pubn/popn/smd2008.pdf> (accessed 20 April 2010).

5
"The Morning After": Understanding and Exploring the Psychosocial Impact of the Women's Charter on Families Experiencing Domestic Violence

Sudha Nair

Introduction

Family violence is a complex issue relating to the breakdown of an intimate relationship. Former Senior District Judge Richard Magnus (2003) recognizes family violence as:

> ... a complex criminal offence that has the seriousness of a stranger-to-stranger crime but involves a victim and a perpetrator who know and care for one another. A person subject to family violence in the home is no less a victim than a person beaten on the sidewalk in front of the home. The law does not stop at the front door of the family home.

In the last fourteen years, the amendments to the Singapore Women's Charter have tightened the law to accord not only more protection for victims, but also help for families through the provision of counselling orders. At the same time, there have been efforts to increase public awareness and interagency networking initiatives at the macro level to address this problem.

In situations of family violence, the perpetrators of violence find themselves in a peculiar and contradictory situation. In the aftermath of the violent act, the perpetrators, seeing the outcome of the violence, are forced to confront the truth of their vicious nature. However, they invariably cannot accept it and end up dismissing it. They are unable to make sense of their violence and to place it in terms of a reality they can live with (Eisikovits and Buchbinder 2000).

Contrary to the popular notion that family violence ends in the break-up of marriages, most couples in a violent relationship in Singapore have been found to want to save their marriages. An evaluation study of the Mandatory Counselling Programme commissioned by the Ministry of Community Development, Youth and Sports (MCYS) in 2004 indicated that seven out of ten survivors of violence stated that their lives had improved and decided to remain in their marriages after undergoing the programmes (MCYS 2007*a*, *b*). However there are also instances where the couples may decide the marriage is not worth saving and end up in divorce or separation. The law, by and large, has had a positive impact on families experiencing violence. However, there have been instances where the law has had unintended consequences on these families. When this happens, the family suffers additional stress.

This chapter seeks to understand the impact the Singapore Women's Charter has on families experiencing violence. In gathering data, a phenomenological approach, which involves understanding the situation as people experience it, was adopted. In other words, to understand the impact of laws and policies on families experiencing violence, one needs to understand it in the context of their reality. This chapter will discuss access issues in family violence cases, maintenance, and gaps in the current system that need to be addressed. To illustrate the key points in this chapter, a case study analysis with case illustrations from PAVe, the Centre for Promoting Alternatives to Violence, will be used.

The Significance of the Amendments to the Women's Charter on Social Services in Singapore

The setting up of the Family Court and the amendments to the Women's Charter in 1995 and 1996 respectively turned out to be a real boon for the social services sector. For the first time, social workers could reach out to the entire family experiencing violence in the confines of the home — these included survivors, abusers, and child witnesses. In addition, the widening of the laws to include family members has also allowed for issues of sibling violence, child-to-parent abuse, and the perpetration of elder abuse to gain attention. The widened definition of the family that goes beyond spouses and children to include in-laws and ex-spouses, as well as the inclusion of psychological and emotional abuse in the definition of family violence, allows for more members of the family to seek protection.

At the same time, the setting up of community-based services through Family Service Centres (FSCs), specialized services such as the Centre for Promoting Alternatives to Violence (PAVe) in 1999, SAFE @ TRANS in 2003, and the Centre for Family Harmony in 2006, complemented what the law provides. This collaborative justice (Magnus 2006) is critical, especially in areas of family violence. Services should complement the laws to provide follow-up aid, since where the law ends, the services must continue. Through an initiative between the Family Court and PAVe in 1999, community justice was served in the heartlands where families experiencing violence were able to apply for Personal Protection Orders (PPOs) through video-linked services in the community, that is, near their homes. There are currently three more centres[1] which provide this service. The amendments to the Women's Charter did not directly cause this development. However, it was the greater publicity and realization that services need to be made more accessible to the community that helped to make community justice a reality.

The revisions to the Women's Charter also yielded an unintended positive consequence — it opened doors to people who were not mandated to receive counselling. The services saw an increase in people coming forward voluntarily to deal with issues of violence, simply because efforts of outreach were made available to the public. Figures taken from PAVe of new cases over a five-year period exemplify this trend (see Table 5.1).

Table 5.1

Breakdown of Mandatory and Voluntary Cases from PAVe, 2002/03–2007/08

Financial Year	Total Number of Cases	No. of Mandatory Cases / No. of Voluntary Cases	Percentage of Mandatory Cases / Percentage of Voluntary Cases	Percentage change
2002/03	373	265	71%	—
		108	29%	—
2003/04	547	357	65%	+34.7%
		190	35%	−75.9%
2004/05	374	197	53%	−44.8%
		177	47%	+6.8%
2005/06	334	162	49%	−17.8%
		172	51%	+2.8%
2006/07	316	145	46%	−10.5%
		171	54%	+0.6%
2007/08	451	179	40%	−23.4%
		272	60%	+59.1%

Source: PAVe (2002/03–2007/08).

The changes in the legislation also brought forth a realization that child welfare and family violence need to be seen in tandem because of the co-relationship between family violence and child maltreatment (Edelson 2001; Postmus and Ortega 2005).

In 1995, the police networking pilot scheme was established. It saw the police and family service agencies working together to provide early help to victims of violence. The success of the pilot scheme led to the setting up of an Integrated Management of Family Violence system in Singapore in 1997 (MCYS 2007*b*). This system has given recognition to the need for a multidisciplinary, integrated, and collaborative partnership between the police, the legal system, the health system, the education system, and the social services system in the management of family violence in Singapore. What this implicitly did was to make family violence a public issue — it was no longer seen as a private family matter.

Another amendment that was significant to survivors of violence was related to breaches of PPO. With the amendment, breaches of PPO constituted a seizable offence, indicating to the perpetrator the seriousness of recalcitrant behaviour. With these amendments, once a report of a breach is filed, the police can take further action because the breaches come under the Penal Code.

While the intent of the Women's Charter is evident, families experiencing violence have encountered difficulties when attempting to negotiate the system. The following sections detail the various scenarios that families have encountered.

The Women's Charter: Consequences for Families Experiencing Violence

Women still continue to form the largest group of survivors of interpersonal violence. Global figures indicate that between 15 and 71 per cent of women report physical abuse by an intimate partner at least once during their lifetime (WHO 2005). In Singapore, 69 per cent of cases registered with the Family Court in 2004 were cases of spousal violence (Family & Juvenile Justice Division, Subordinate Court 2005). Of this, 82 per cent of the applicants for PPOs at the Subordinate Court comprised women. While this chapter acknowledges that men may also be victims of violence, it will focus primarily on the experiences of women and children.

Family Violence Cases and the Enforcement of Maintenance Orders

The issue of maintenance has received attention in Parliament (Singapore Parliamentary Debates 2008, 2009), especially in relation to non-compliance of orders. The concern is valid, especially in relation to the impact a lack of finances has on women, especially those in the lower income group. Research shows that women in a violent relationship who are dependent on their husband for support become poorer when they leave the relationship (Postmus and Hahn 2007; Brush 2004).

It was reported by the Minister for Community Development, Youth and Sports that in 2007, there were about 6,300 applications for maintenance orders, out of which more than half, that is, 54 per cent (3,450) were for the enforcement of existing orders. Dr Mohammad Maliki Osman, Parliamentary Secretary to the Ministry for National Development, estimated that based on divorce statistics, there are possibly at least 5,000 children below the age of eighteen who are affected by divorce every year (Singapore Parliamentary Debates 2009). For women in a violent relationship who have chosen to apply for maintenance, the non-compliance of the maintenance orders intensifies the hardship many of them go through. The following case studies illustrate the struggles of two women in their attempt to navigate the maintenance system.

Janna[2] related how she tried to enforce the maintenance order twice, but each time her husband was given a chance to put in the money, he never did. After two attempts, she gave up because pursuing the enforcement meant having to take three of her five children, aged between two and five years, to the courts each time her husband defaulted on payment. Making trips to the court was tiring because she had to bring her three children with her and they used public transport. Moreover, the process was draining owing to her repeated visits to the Family Court. Finally, she decided to give up. Ironically, her ex-husband continues to live in the same flat. He also lives off the income of $300 she receives from renting out a room. In spite of having a job, he does not contribute to the household income. The family struggles; her older children receive help from the School Pocket Money Fund. Janna also receives food rations from social service agencies. Here is how she describes her struggles:

> [*I feel like*] I need to beg for money. It is very hard because institutions say they need a divorce certificate [to qualify for financial aid as a single parent]. It angers

> me when I see that he has a remittance card [sending
> money overseas]. He doesn't pay me at all yet he
> eats the food I cook and expects me to take care of
> his needs. I only live with $300 a month because my
> other tenant left. Living everyday is hard. I can't get
> any cent from him no matter what I try.

June went twenty-two times to court to get her maintenance.
Her husband did not meet the deadline several times. On two
occasions, his lawyers paid the maintenance when the date
was due. At other times, he would default, and when she
went to enforce the order, he would deposit the money the
night before the next deadline. Sometimes he would deposit
small amounts, but the following month he would default
again. When she attempted to get help from social service
organizations for her children's education, she was told to
enforce the order. After the eighteenth time, she asked for
an attachment order, but he protested and she was told by
professionals that his job would be affected if she pursued it
and she would not get anything from him. In one instance,
he also made her account for all the money that she spent
on the children. Since then, she has returned to the court
for the twenty-third time with a request for an attachment
order,[3] but her request was still not granted. She explains
her dilemma:

> I wish I didn't have to ask for maintenance. I am tired.
> I have been supporting him and the two kids, two cars
> plus rent plus maid. I worked very hard [during the
> marriage]. I feel so burnt out. Every month, I have to
> ask for maintenance. I wish I didn't need it. I feel it
> more now because I used to support him. To go and
> ask for bursary for my kids — when their father is

> doing so well. I am torn. I am stuck. He wants to pay
> for access[4] but can't pay for maintenance. He always
> has excuses. He went for mediation and told them
> he'd pay. Then he pays in dribs and drabs. I'm so
> tired ... I feel so low ... sometimes I feel I want to
> give up totally ...

While the woman and her children are no longer victims of physical violence, on issues of maintenance, economic abuse persists. Economic abuse is defined as "preventing the partner from getting or keeping a job; making a partner ask for money, allocating an allowance, taking partner's or ex's money; not informing or limiting access to family income" (Domestic Abuse Intervention Project 1993, m-ed 7h02). This is where money is used as a means to perpetuate the sense of power the perpetrator has over the victim, who is not allowed to have a job so as to ensure her continual dependence on him. Or, when the victims have a job, their salaries are handed over to their spouses who expect them to live off small sums, sometimes forcing them to beg for more. The very act of having to go for repeated enforcements, and having to account for every cent she spends, is tantamount to psychological and economic abuse.

Oftentimes, the victim gives up pursuing the enforcement of the order or, in some instances, continues attempting to enforce the order out of desperation for financial survival. However, the continuous appearance in court becomes tiring, and many women eventually give up. In addition, the legal fees are often unaffordable, especially for women who do not qualify for legal aid or pro-bono legal aid. In this case, some women end up representing themselves. For these women, other financial help is not forthcoming because of the presence of the maintenance order. Hence, it is not surprising that they tend to slip into financial hardship. However, what is most frustrating for women experiencing violence and not receiving the maintenance due to them, is that the onus for ensuring the maintenance is paid is dependent on the survivors taking the non-compliant spouse to task. Making sure that the non-compliant party pays up is particularly complex in a violent relationship since the nature of the relationship is one of power and control of the perpetrator over the victim.

From a family violence perspective, therefore, the refusal of perpetrators to make payments and the continuous attempts to enforce orders weaken the victims' mental and physical resolve. It results in what Biderman refers to as "induced debility and exhaustion" (Biderman 1957; see also Condonis, Paroissien and Aldrich 1990) — a technique used by captors who torture prisoners of war into compliance. In the same vein, non-compliance of maintenance orders allows the perpetrator to maintain the level of control he had over the family.

As a result of the obstacles the victims' face, many may end up in serial marriages in an attempt to receive emotional support and attain economic stability (Singapore Parliamentary Debates 2009). Such a trend can lead to increased dysfunctionality in families.

An unintended consequence is the impact on children observing the processes as they follow their mothers to court or experience the frustrations their mothers feel. This may result in resentment of their fathers whom they see as not caring about their needs. This is especially so when the children are mature enough and able to discern issues of fairness and parity. A systemic reaction is that when the perpetrators apply for access and when maintenance is not paid, the children resist access arrangements because, in their minds, access and maintenance are interrelated and indicate the other person's care and concern for their needs.

Family Violence and Its Impact on Children

The impact of family violence on children has been well documented (Holden and Ritchie 1991; Hughes 1998; Rossman 2001; Edleson 2004). In a review of articles about childhood exposure to interpersonal conflict, Grych and Fincham (1990) found that marital discord in families had an impact on the adjustment of children and that adjustment problems actually became more pronounced with increased exposure to interparental conflict. In homes where violence occurs, children are exposed to continuous, day-to-day "terrorism" (Johnson 1995, p. 284). Like their mothers, they also never know when the next episode of violence is going to occur (Nair, Pang and Soh 2001). In a study conducted by the Family Court of Singapore in 2004, it was found that of the entire caseload heard in court, 32 per cent involved children. In terms of profile, 61 per cent of the children were under the age of ten and 68 per cent were hurt in the process of trying to intervene (Subordinate Court 2004, Issue 38).

In responding to a landmark ruling on *PP v Luan Yuanxin* (SLR 2, 2002, p. 98), then Chief Justice Yong Pung How commented:

> Violent acts such as these are particularly heinous when they are committed within the confines of familial relationships as they constitute an abuse of the bonds of trust and interdependency that exist between family members. More often than not, the effects of such violence within the family fall most harshly upon the children who, while they may not be the direct recipients of the violence, will nevertheless carry the scars of these acts of brutality.

In an unpublished study on child witnesses of violence, Nair (2006) found that many adolescents recalled seeing the first incidents of violence perpetrated by one parent against the other when they were between the ages of three and six. Many of these incidents remained vividly etched on their minds. Because of this, the granting of access, supervised or unsupervised, to a child growing up in a violent home — especially where the perpetrator has not accepted responsibility and accountability for his behaviour — is "frightening" from a child's perspective.

Having been exposed to violence from a very early age and having role models who provide little structure in terms of dealing with conflict, some children may grow up viewing violence as an acceptable form of solving problems (Fagan 2005). The literature on this, however, is clear, that is, it is erroneous to assume that all children who grow up exposed to domestic violence will end up being abusive themselves because research shows that exposure to violence and subsequent perpetration of violence is a complex issue (Choice, Danokoski, Keiley, Llyod, Seery and Thomas 2006). Other factors, such as the extent of individual resilience (Marsten 2001; Marsten and Powell

2003; Luthar, Cicchetti and Becker 2000), the presence of a caring adult, individual personality and temperament (Osofsky 1999), and the child's social support network, control, beliefs and coping behaviours (Osofsky 1998; Rossman, Hughes and Rosenberg 1999), and attachment to formal institutions (Akers 1998), can make a difference to the outcome for a child.

The Women's Charter addresses issues of violence, custody, and access, but these are treated as discrete issues. Obviously, where children are concerned, the court has made their welfare a primary concern. In 2008, the Family and Child Care Court[5] was set up within the Subordinate Court, Family and Juvenile Division to ensure that children's voices are heard. However, children and parents have alluded to facing challenges in accessing the system. The following section describes some of these challenges.

Access Issues Prior to a Custody Order

In the average custody dispute case where access is an issue, children are often caught in acrimonious situations between warring parents. In most divorce cases, the Women's Charter recognizes the importance of mutual parental responsibility in relation to custody (Ong 2003) and access to the child. However in a violent relationship that ends in the break-up of a marriage, inevitably issues of custody and access have to be considered (Wolak and Finklehor 1998). There will be questions about the future safety of children in the custody of an abusive father, and consideration of the possible contact between the abused woman and the abusive man, which could put the former at risk (Wolak and Finklehor 1998).

When the child is either a victim and/or witness to the abuse of one parent by the other, and then access to the child is given to the abusive parent, this is a double whammy for the child. He/she does not only have to deal with the acrimony between the parents, but also the fear of being left with the parent perpetrating the violence. The following cases detail the experiences of two children attending supervised access sessions at a social service agency.

Mark, aged seven, a victim of violence, describes his experience of the supervised access sessions that he was ordered to attend by the court:

> I'm so afraid every time we go. I try to go to the toilet as I want to get away from the room, and, when I go home, I always have very bad headaches the whole day and at night I cannot sleep. Every time we [brother and himself] do something he [father] did not like, he would become like the Incredible Hulk, except that he does not turn Green, he turns Red. At school, I'm so worried that Daddy will come and snatch me and I will not see Mummy and my brother again. I have a PPO but no one can help me.

Other children have alluded to the fact that their views are not heard. Twelve-year-old Ryan describes how his father, the abusive parent, continued to put him down during the supervised access sessions. He told counsellors and the court about his father losing his temper during the sessions and that he was fearful of seeing his father again. However, instead of his father being mandated to receive counselling to deal with his anger, Ryan was mandated for counselling instead. Clearly, Ryan was confused by the decision of the court. In his own words:

> We [my brother and I] have done no wrong, yet we
> are being sent for counselling, and he has the anger
> issues and when he refuses to go for counselling,
> nothing happens to him.

The Convention of the Rights of the Child makes explicit
reference to giving children a voice and listening to their
views. Article 12 of the Convention of the Rights of the
Child[6] states that:

1. Parties shall assure to the child who is capable of forming
   his or her own views the right to express those views
   freely in all matters affecting the child, the views of the
   child being given due weight in accordance with the age
   and maturity of the child.
2. For this purpose, the child shall in particular be
   provided the opportunity to be heard in any judicial and
   administrative proceedings affecting the child, either
   directly, or through a representative or an appropriate
   body, in a manner consistent with the procedural rules
   of national law.

It is important to reiterate here that the Family Court has
put in place systems to hear the children's wishes. However
as pointed out in a paper presented by the Family and
Juvenile Justice Division in 2005, these issues are not
straightforward. At all times, what governs decisions is
the principle of the best interest of the child.

In the case discussed above, it is prudent to note that
the child was open to access, if his father dealt with the
violence and accepted accountability for his action. From a
family violence perspective, two things are likely to occur
if there is no change in the father's behaviour. One, as trust

has clearly been broken, the child is perpetually in a state of hypervigilance whenever access visits are due because he perceives that if he behaves in any way other than what his father expects, he will be hurt. The manifestations of these behaviours, however, can become internalized, as in the case of Mark who suffers from headaches, sleeplessness, and withdrawal symptoms. Second, children also externalize their behaviours by taking out their anger on others, for example, confronting the perpetrator during access sessions. This occurs especially among adolescents. In Ryan's case, for example, he allegedly confronted his father, who in turn, allegedly accused the boy of being instigated by other adults. Other common external manifestations are: increased behavioural infractions such as lying, stealing, and aggressive behaviours that inevitably bring them to the attention of the authorities. Several studies have identified these internalized and externalized behaviours which vary by developmental stages (Hughes 1998; Jaffe, Wolfe, Wilson and Zak 1986; Moore and Peplar 1998).

In Singapore, the law is generally in favour of joint-parental responsibility (Leong 2007; Ong 2003) for the custody of children, except in instances where there are occurrences of family violence in which children have been physically, emotionally, or sexually abused; or, there is such acrimony between the parents that despite mediation and counselling, they are unable to put aside their differences, and their inability to cooperate would be detrimental to the child (Ong 2003). This is important as it recognizes that there are situations where children can be even more impacted by warring parents. But how much of the experiences of children are taken into account when decisions are made?

How do we balance parental rights and responsibilities with the child's rights and best interests? Do protection and custody/access issues need to be heard in the same court before a decision is made to leave a child/children with the abusive parent? This makes sense as the history of the child's experiences in relation to the violence cited can then be considered, and appropriate measures taken to ensure that the parents make attempts to build up the trust and the relationship.

Removal of Children: Who Is Being Punished?

The Women's Charter and the Children and Young Persons Act (CYPA) need to be considered together on issues of family violence, although children's exposure (both witnessing and experiencing) to violence is covered under the latter Act. Children exposed to violence face the possibility of being removed from their homes and committed to a place of safety provided for under the CYPA. Their parents, in turn, face a real threat of losing custody of their children to child protection services because of their inability to resolve the abuse (Buzawa and Buzawa 2003). Unfortunately, this poses a dilemma for the victimized woman and, in turn, this fear hinders her from seeking help because she does not want to lose her children. There are no available statistics to track situations of children's removal on these grounds. Two different courts are involved in such cases — the Family Court and the Juvenile Court. While the courts' main concern is the safety of the child, from the children's perspective, their removal from the parental home is perceived as a punishment for an act committed by an adult family member. In this case, they come to see themselves as having no control over their own lives. Their sense of powerlessness is reinforced by the very system set up to help them. The following case studies illustrate this point.

Two sets of siblings related how they felt they were punished for their father's abusive behaviour. Stella, aged fourteen, and Jacob, aged twelve, were removed from their parents after their mother was severely abused by their father. They were then aged five and three years respectively. Having lived in several foster homes since their removal, they pondered their future. Describing themselves as "birds in a cage", they wondered for how long they would have to "pay" for their father's behaviour. He was living in their home, but they had not had a home to call their own since pre-school years. Their father continues to abuse their mother and has not taken responsibility for his behaviour.

In the second case, Kim Seng, was first sent to a "residential home" at age ten. His mother had left their home with the children after his father used a chopper to threaten them. She rented a room with a friend and could not take the children with her. She, therefore, approached social services for help and the children were placed in a residential institution[7] on compassionate grounds. Kim Seng felt punished for something he had not done and started acting up in the "residential home". This resulted in his being punished by his losing privileges such as home leave. Eventually, he was sent to a closed institution.[8] However, this only served to intensify his anger. The real cause of his behaviour was never explored.

The laws, in effect, are meant to protect children and adults; yet while they protect and are oftentimes empowering, they can also work against the rights of innocent victims whose lives go awry because of the behaviour of adults who choose to use violence in their relationships. In this case, should society not be asking questions such as, whose needs are we really serving when we remove the child? What sanctions are in place for the perpetrators to ensure that their behaviours change so that the children can return to their homes? What happens when the perpetrators refuse to change? Does the child continue to remain in foster care and/or institutions until he reaches adulthood while the perpetrating parent continues to stay in his/her home? And, as the children rightly put it, why is the onus of responsibility on them to behave well when nothing they do makes a difference in changing their circumstances? How do we balance the risks to children with parental capability and responsibility?

Breaches of Personal Protection Orders (PPOs)

As stated earlier in this chapter, breaches of the PPOs are seizable offences under the Penal Code. This amendment, which allows for survivors of violence to get immediate help, was lauded when the law was first amended in 1996. Prior to the amendments, a woman would have to be abused first, then apply for the PPO, and be abused a second time before she could apply for an attachment of a powers of arrest to the PPO. The woman would then have to be beaten a third time before the powers of arrest would be activated and a warrant of arrest issued. All this changed after the amendments. Survivors of violence can now feel secure that the amendments in the law protect them against repeated abuse. In obvious and serious cases, especially in instances where physical abuse occurs, action is swift and the law "kicks in" quickly. When issues are not so clearly defined, however, the process of obtaining help can be excruciatingly difficult. The following case study demonstrates this point.

Leng left her home after her husband abused her. She obtained a PPO and lived in a shelter for a while. She eventually got a job and managed to reorganize her life. However, her husband tracked her down. He stalked her regularly at her workplace and created a scene each time, so much so that her bosses had to transfer her to a different outlet. But this did not deter him. Somehow he would always find her and appear at her workplace. As a frontline worker, his presence at her workplace affected her job. The police were called in several times, but action was difficult to pursue. He either put on a very pathetic front with the police or disappeared when they arrived. There was no physical violence. However, he followed her home, constantly called her colleagues to ask about her, and turned up at her workplace. As a result of her husband's behaviour, she risked losing her job. She was highly stressed and in a constant state of hypervigilance. In her frustration she said:

> What is the point of having a PPO, when the police cannot do anything. He sees no consequence to his behaviour and he is continuing to harass me.

While the laws are in place, their implementation appears difficult and abused survivors feel unsupported. In this case, for all the husband's "pathetic" appearance, the fact remains that he continually harassed Leng. Despite the recognition of psychological abuse in the law, there is still a tendency for the public and professionals alike to undermine psychological abuse in relation to what is more obvious — physical abuse (MCYS 2007*a*). What follows is that victims stop reporting infractions as they perceive that no action will be taken and the feeling of helplessness prevails (Walker 2000).

When action is taken and perpetrators are incarcerated for breaches of PPO, social workers have reported that often the sentences are too short, usually less than a year, and that the prison lacks programmes for rehabilitating short-term offenders. Thus for recalcitrant offenders, the system becomes a "revolving door", with abuse recurring, followed by short sentences and repeated offences. In this case, questions arise as to whether the law is effective as a deterrent for recalcitrant offenders. While the law may be there, the will to change clearly must come from the offender, and the message that the legal system sends out should highlight the seriousness of the offence.

Personal Protection Orders (PPOs) and Partner Relationships

The exclusion of partners or cohabitees from the definition of family violence is a growing concern. While there is general recognition of the moral question of what constitutes a family, the safety and protection for the woman in a cohabitation relationship are a cause for concern, as the dynamics involved are no different from those of a woman in a marital relationship. Seen from the context of protection and safety, intimate partner violence — although the relationship of the parties involved is not legally recognized — is, nevertheless, as serious as violence experienced by partners in a legal matrimonial relationship.

One of the worst cases of cohabitee violence in Singapore was a thirty-eight-year-old woman whose partner of six years was a fifty-six-year-old man with whom she had two children. In the relationship, she had suffered massive physical abuse: she was blinded, slashed, as well as sexually and psychologically abused. Despite several attempts to seek assistance at the earlier stages of the abuse, there was no protection available to her because of her cohabitee status. She approached family service centres, shelters, the police, and even the courts, but help was limited. Eventually, she was found in an emaciated, semi-conscious state when her then three-year-old child opened the door to a young police officer who had responded to a tip-off from a grassroots leader. The perpetrator was sentenced to seven-and-a-half years' jail and nine strokes of the cane. On his release from prison, he sought her out and the abuse continued. He was charged again and sentenced to three months' imprisonment. The additional trauma she had suffered because of the continued beatings resulted in her being unable to remember details of the incidents, which made it difficult for the police to prosecute him further.

This case study questions the kind of protection accorded to women in a partner relationship. Many do not come forward for help because of the recognition that help is not forthcoming. The Women's Charter is clear about what constitutes a family in Singapore (Leong 2007). Evidently the laws protecting women are bound to what is deemed moral, and reflect the values of the larger society. That the law does not adequately provide protection to every woman is a cause for concern, particularly since society is fast changing and non-legal relationships are on the increase. Instead of being a moral code, the law should ideally be focused on protecting the life and rights of individuals, which is tantamount to protecting all women, irrespective of how they live their private lives.

Conclusion

The narratives in this chapter illustrate the dilemmas faced by women and children experiencing violence. Clearly more research needs to be done to establish the extent of the problems faced by these survivors so that laws, programmes, and services may be strengthened to help them better.

The Women's Charter is undoubtedly a piece of legislation with noble intentions to protect all women, including victims of violence. According to the law, the family is defined in strict moral terms, covering only individuals who are married to each other. Women who choose to live with partners are left out of the law completely. In this regard, the law is restrictive as it does not take into account changing trends in society — such as alternative family arrangements where individuals cohabit with each other — and protect the rights of these individuals. In this sense, the law is more concerned about preserving the family than protecting the rights of individuals, notably women in this case. Because women in partner relationships do experience domestic violence, there is a need for the law to be extended to cover them as well.

From the discussion, it is clear that adults in a violent relationship have the option of leaving the home in search of safety. It is a choice they make as to whether to stay or leave the home. But the choices of children as dependents also need to be taken into account. Instead in many instances, the law dictates the removal of children, a drastic experience for the children involved, especially if alternative care is not available. Here, the children are doubly victimized and unable to exercise choices. In this case, much more thought should go into how the implementation of the law can better provide protection for children without robbing them of their rights. At the same time, we need to find a balance between the risk to children and parental capability and responsibility.

Maintenance orders are meant to ensure that both parents exercise parental responsibility. However, when it comes to the enforcement of maintenance orders, the responsibility falls on the survivors to take steps to ensure compliance. This lopsided situation reinforces the power that the perpetrators have over their partners. Perhaps there is also a need to rethink the onus and rights of both parents in the enforcement of these orders.

The Women's Charter clearly has a significant role in protecting women's rights. Further enhancements to the law and implementation efforts would result in a richer piece of legislation. In addition, there is the issue of individual responsibility. Real change, commitment, and a sense of responsibility and accountability for their behaviour can only come from the perpetrators of violence themselves.

Notes

1. These are SAFE @ TRANS, Loving Heart, and the Syariah Court.
2. The names used throughout the chapter are pseudonyms to protect the identities of the women and children who were interviewed.
3. The attaching of earnings order is where the court orders the employer to deduct the maintenance payment directly from the non-compliant spouse's salary.
4. In this case, her husband had the right to pay for supervised access sessions at a social service agency.
5. See also Subordinate Court, "Family Violence: Perspectives of the Singapore Family Court", 2006. Available at <http:// app.subcourts.gov.sg>, this article provides a list of the programmes available to families experiencing violence. See also Magnus and Wong's (2005) paper, "The Role of Judicial Process in Child Protection: A Singaporean Perspective". This is also available at <http://www.app. subcourts.gov.sg> (accessed 12 May 2009).
6. "Convention of the Rights of the Child" <http//www.unicef. org/crc/index_30177.html> (accessed 12 May 2009).
7. A residential institution is a juvenile facility, run either by MCYS or a voluntary welfare organization, for young persons below the age of sixteen who are in need of care and control. It can be an open institution which allows children and young persons to attend school and other activities, while staying in the home.
8. Closed institutions are juvenile institutions where children and young persons who have committed deliquent acts are admitted under a court order. Once admitted, the children and young persons are required to complete their term, as set out in the court order. After meeting a portion of their

order with good behaviour, they may be given schooling privileges.

References

Akers, R.L. *Social Learning and Social Structure: A General Theory of Crime and Deviance.* Boston, M.A.: Northeastern University Press, 1998.

Biderman, A.D. "Communist Attempts to Elicit False Confessions from Air Force Prisoners of War". *Bulletin of the New York Academy of Medicine* 33, no. 9 (1957): 616–25.

Brush, L.D. "Battering and the Poverty Trap". *Journal of Poverty* 8, no. 3 (2004): 23–43.

Buzawa, E.S and C.G. Buzawa. *Domestic Violence: The Criminal Justice Response.* Thousand Oaks, California: Sage Publications, 2003.

Choice, P., M.E. Danokoski, M.K. Keiley, S.A. Lloyd, B.L. Seery, and V. Thomas. "Affect Regulation and the Cycle of Violence Against Women: New Directions for Understanding the Process". *Journal of Family Violence* 21 (2006): 327–39.

Condonis, M., K. Paroissien, and B. Aldrich. *The Mutual Help Group — A Therapeutic Programme for Women Who Have Been Abused.* New South Wales: Redfern Legal Centre Publishing, 1990.

"Convention of the Rights of the Child". <http://www.unicef.org/crc/index_30177.html> (accessed 12 May 2009).

Domestic Abuse Intervention Project. *The Cycle of Violence.* Duluth, Minnesota, 1993.

Edelson, J.L. "Should Children's Exposure to Adult Domestic Violence Be Defined as Child Maltreatment Under the Law?" In *Protecting Children from Domestic Violence: Strategies for Community Intervention*, edited by P.J. Jaffe,

L.L. Baker, and A.J. Cunningham. New York: The Guilford House, 2004.

————. "Studying the Co-occurrence of Child Maltreatment and Domestic Violence in Families". In *Domestic Violence in the Lives of Children: The Future of Research, Intervention and Social Policy,* edited by S. Graham-Bermann and J. Edelson. Washington, D.C: American Psychological Association, 2001.

Eisikovits, Z. and E. Buchbinder. *Locked in a Violent Embrace: Understanding and Intervening in Domestic Violence.* Thousand Oaks, California: Sage Publications, 2000.

Fagan, A.A. "The Relationship between Adolescent Physical Abuse and Criminal Offending: Support for an Enduring and Generalised Cycle of Violence". *Journal of Family Violence* 20, no. 5 (2005): 279–90.

Family & Juvenile Justice Division, Subordinate Court. "Hearing Children's Wishes: Practice of the Singapore Family Court in Divorce Proceedings". Paper presented at "International Forum on Family Relationships: Legislative and Policy Responses". Canberra, Australia, 2005.

Grych, J.H. and F.D. Fincham. "Marital Conflict and Children's Adjustment: A Cognitive-Contextual Framework". *Psychological Bulletin* 108 (1990): 267–90.

Holden, G.W. and K.L. Ritchie. "Linking Extreme Marital Discord, Child Rearing, and Child Behavior Problems: Evidence from Battered Women". *Child Development* 62 (1991): 311–27.

Hughes, H.M. "Psychological and Behavioural Correlates of Family Violence in Child Witnesses and Victims". *American Journal of Orthopsychiatry* 58 (1998): 77–90.

Jaffe, P., D. Wolfe, D.A. Wilson, and L. Zak. "Psychological Functioning of Children in a Battered Women's Shelter: A Comparative Analysis of Girls and Boys Behavioural

Symptoms". *American Journal of Psychiatry* 143 (1986): 73–77.

Johnson, M.P. "Patriarchal Terrorism and Common Couple Violence: Two Forms of Violence against Women". *Journal of Marriage and the Family* 57 (1995): 283–94.

Leong Wai Kum. *Elements of Family Law in Singapore*. Singapore. LexisNexis, 2007.

Luthar, S.S., D. Cicchetti, and B. Becker. "The Construct of Resilience: A Critical Evaluation and Guidelines for Future Work". *Child Development* 71 (2000): 543–62.

Magnus, R. "The Citizenship of the Family Justice Process", 2006. <http://app.subcourts.gov.sg> (accessed 12 May 2009).

———. "Violence in the Family". *Law Gazette*, 2003. <http://www.lawgazette.com.sg/2003-10/Oct03-feature.htm> (accessed 19 May 2009).

Magnus, R. and L.T. Wong. "The Role of Judicial Process in Child Protection: A Singaporean Perspective", 2005. <http://www.app.subcourts.gov.sg> (accessed 12 May 2009).

Marsten, A.S. "Ordinary Magic: Resilience Processes in Development". *American Psychologist* 53, no. 2 (2001): 205–20.

Marsten, A.S. and J.L. Powell. "A Resilience Framework". In *Resilience and Vulnerability: Adaptation in the Context of Childhood Adversities*, edited by S.S. Luthar. Cambridge: Cambridge University Press, 2003.

Ministry of Community Development, Youth and Sports (MCYS). *Protecting Families from Violence*. Singapore, 2007a.

———. *Integrated Management of Family Violence System in Singapore*. Singapore, 2007b.

Moore, T.E. and D.J. Peplar. "Corelates of Adjustment in Children at Risk". In *Children Exposed to Marital Violence: Theories, Research and Applied Issues*, edited by G.W. Holden, R. Geffner, and E.N. Jouriles. Washington, D.C.: American Psychological Association, 1998.

Nair, Sudha. "Growing up with Family Violence: The Life Stories of Juvenile Delinquents and their Siblings". Unpublished doctoral thesis. Department of Social Work, National University of Singapore, 2006.

Nair, S., K.T. Pang, and S.F. Soh. "Children's Resilience in Living in Violent Families". *Asia-Pacific Journal of Social Work* 11 (2001): 63–77.

Ong, D.S.L. "Making No Custody Order: Re G (Guardianship of an Infant)". *Singapore Journal of Legal Studies* (2003): 583–92.

Osofsky, J.D. "The Impact of Violence on Children". *The Future of Children Journal* 9 (Special Issue), no. 3 (1999): 33–49.

———. "Children as Invisible Victims of Domestic and Community Violence". In *Children Exposed to Domestic Violence: Theory, Research and Applied Issues*, edited by G.W. Holden, R. Geffner, and E.N. Jouriles. Washington, D.C.: American Psychological Association, 1998.

Postmus, J.L. and D. Ortega. "Serving Two Masters: When Domestic Violence and Child Abuse Overlap". *Families in Society* 86, no. 4 (2005): 483–90.

Postmus, J.L. and S.A. Hahn. "The Collaboration between Welfare and Advocacy Organizations: Learning from the Experiences of Domestic Violence Survivors". *Families in Society* 88, no. 3 (2007): 475–84.

Rossman, B.B.R. "Longer Term Effects of Children's Exposure to Domestic Violence". In *Domestic in the Lives of Children: The Future of Research, Intervention and Social Policy*, edited by S.A. Graham-Bermann and J.L. Edelson. Washington, D.C.: American Psychological Association, 2001.

Rossman, B.B.R., H.M. Hughes, and M.S. Rosenberg. *Children and Interparental Violence: The Impact of Exposure*. Washington, D.C.: Brunner/Mazel, 1999.

Singapore Parliamentary Debates (2008). Official Report for 26 May 2008. <http://www.parliament.gov.sg> (accessed 12 May 2009).

Singapore Parliamentary Debates (2009). Official Report for 11 February 2009. <http://www.parliament.gov.sg> (accessed 12 May 2009).

Subordinate Court. "Family Violence: Perspectives of the Singapore Family Court", 2006. <http://www.app.subcourts. gov.sg> (accessed 12 May 2009).

————. "The Many Faces of Family Violence". *Research Bulletin* 38, 2004.

Walker, L.E. *The Battered Woman's Syndrome.* New York: Springer, 2000.

Wolak, J. and D. Finklehor. *Partner Violence: A Comprehensive Review of 20 Years of Research.* Thousand Oaks, California: Sage Publications, 1998.

World Health Organization (WHO). *Addressing Violence Against Women and Achieving the Millennium Development Goals,* 2005.

Legislative Documents

Public Prosecutor v Luan Yuanxin. SLR 2 (2002): 98 at 103.

6
Epilogue: Some Thoughts on Protecting Women's Rights in the Family and Beyond

Theresa W. Devasahayam

Women's rights in countries the world over are protected by a gamut of laws. There are pieces of legislation enabling women's participation in the public sphere or civil society and the arenas of education, mass media, market economy, and politics. There are also laws protecting women's rights in the private sphere of the family. Family practices on the role and authority of the father in the family, obligations and duties of both husband and wife, divorce, inheritance rules, child custody, and other related issues are all governed by laws. Civil family and marriage legislation found in the different countries in Southeast Asia are about correcting the asymmetrical relationship between men and women in their personal lives — an arena where intervention is evidently problematic because it involves interfering in people's private lives.

The Singapore Women's Charter is no different from numerous other marriage and family legislation found in countries in the region. The Charter is about women and men

— their roles, responsibilities, and rights — in the context of family and marriage. Since its promulgation, the Women's Charter has been a landmark legislation, safeguarding women's rights in matters related to marriage, divorce, matrimonial assets, maintenance, and custody of children. Although called the Women's Charter and commonly perceived to be pro-woman, the legislation is gender-neutral, protecting as it does the rights of both women and men in a marital relationship.

In spite of its efficacy, the Women's Charter is not without imperfections. While it protects a spouse, former spouse, child, stepchild, adopted child, parents, parents-in-law, and any other relative or incapacitated individual who is regarded by the court as a member of the family, couples in *de facto* or "informal marriages" are excluded. Another limitation of the Charter is that only the victim of family violence can apply for a protection order; it has been found that in many instances, however, the victim often believes she cannot help herself and, as a result, does not take the necessary action to end the abusive relationship. The Women's Charter falls short in yet another way. The amended Charter makes it mandatory not only for the abuser, but also the victim, to undergo counselling. To this end, the legislation has the potential effect of "blaming the victim". Another shortcoming of the Charter relates to how it has become enforced; procedural guidelines to ensure the effective enforcement of maintenance orders are much needed for: (a) reducing conflict between spouses and ex-spouses about future continuing financial obligations; (b) encouraging shared parental financial responsibility;

and (c) ensuring that the recovery process for maintenance is not overly burdensome, time-consuming, or costly to the individual who has already gone through the effort and expense of obtaining a final maintenance order from the courts (SCWO 2009). In this regard, the enforcement of the law is as critical as the promulgation of the law itself. The goal of enforcement is to achieve compliance with the rule of prescribed behaviour to the degree which Singapore believes it can afford, based on its resources. Here, the law needs to be effectively enforced because social norms are not strong enough; in this case, "law enforcement also may be able to reinforce social norms and thereby indirectly contribute to effective enforcement" (Polinsky and Shavell 1998, p. 42).

As in the legislation protecting women's rights in the family in the other countries in Southeast Asia, there have been several amendments to the Singapore Women's Charter since its promulgation. The year 1996, for example, saw amendments to the Women's Charter Act which broadened the definition of violence to include intimidation, continual harassment, or restraint against one's will, and provided counselling orders for victims. In this matter, the government has taken an interagency approach involving the courts, police, hospitals, and social service agencies to help victims of violence and the perpetrators. These amendments are clearly not only an expression of political will on the part of the state to ensure greater protection to women, but also a recognition that violence against women is a complicated issue, and women's experiences as victims of violence in the context of marriage are not homogenous.

September 2010 saw the announcement of additional proposed amendments to the Charter. The proposed amendments were spurred by the rising divorce rates and the increase in rates of marriage between Singaporeans and foreigners or permanent residents (Sim and Lum 2010). The proposed amendments, aimed at ensuring that divorce men do not default on maintenance payments owed to their former spouses, have arisen from a growing concern over the welfare of children caught in an acrimonious divorce. With the aim of tightening the enforcement of the maintenance orders by the courts, the proposed amendments are targeted at the defaulter in a number of ways. First, the proposed amendments allow the complainant to report maintenance debts to credit bureaus, which question the creditworthiness of the defaulter. Second, courts have the power to order the defaulter to post a banker's guarantee against future defaults, to undergo financial counselling, or to perform community service. Third, the complainant may obtain the defaulter's employment information from the Central Provident Fund Board in order that direct deductions from the defaulter's salary may be transferred to the maintenance complainant. These further amendments also mandate that divorcees intending to remarry need to declare their existing maintenance arrears to their new brides, as a reminder to the new couple of their previous commitments. This condition, moreover, will apply to Muslim couples who go to the Registry of Muslim Marriages as well. In addition, minors and divorcees intending to remarry are mandated to undergo marriage preparation courses under the proposed amendments.

The powers of the court would also be enhanced as a result of these proposed amendments. For example, courts may now order parents to deposit matrimonial assets of a divorcing couple into their children's Children's Development Accounts for future use to safeguard the welfare of the children. Among divorcing couples with children under twenty-one years of age, courts can order mandatory counselling. In cases in which divorcing couples refuse counselling, the court can make orders such as staying divorce proceedings. The court will also have powers over foreign divorces, as now it can make ancillary orders such as the division of matrimonial assets for those wanting a divorce outside Singapore.

While the proposed amendments in the Charter include greater safeguards for ex-spouses and children of the divorcee, restrictions on those intending to marry will be relaxed. Previously the condition for marriage has been that one party of a couple intending to marry should have lived in Singapore for no less than fifteen days. While this condition has been dropped for Singaporeans living abroad or permanent residents wanting to marry in Singapore, it will continue to apply to couples among whom one party is a non-citizen or permanent resident.

In response to the proposed amendments, there was a government call for feedback from the public by the Ministry of Community Development, Youth and Sports (MCYS) to which some 250 individuals and groups reacted with a rejoinder. Both the Association of Women for Action and Research (AWARE) and the Singapore Council of Women's Organisations (SCWO) advised on establishing a central authority to enforce maintenance payments (Leong 2010).

Other responses questioned whether pre-counselling should be made mandatory for specific groups and whether the Women's Charter should be renamed the Family Charter. Interestingly, feedback was also directed at abolishing immunity from prosecution for the spouse accused of rape by the other.

Having said that, reforms to the law are an implicit recognition that laws are not always perfect. That there has been constant reform to the Women's Charter over the last decades shows that laws — their formulation, revision and application — are indicative of larger social and political processes in the way of changing social norms, shifts in attitude towards the vulnerable in society such as children, and transformations in women's consciousness.

For women activists in Singapore, striving for constant legislative reform now and in the future means that "protection for women" is a project in the making (cf. Stivens 2003). As society develops, there is every reason for women to enjoy greater protection, especially in cases where there is increasing acknowledgement on the part of the state to tap on the potential of women and recognize them as equal partners in the development effort. Singapore is a good example. By and large, government policies towards women are based on the concept of equal opportunity since women are treated as members of mainstream society, on equal footing with men, and not as a special interest group with its own unique characteristics and needs.

Clearly the Singapore Women's Charter is a major step forward in protecting women's rights. To make the Charter work to its fullest potential entails that all barriers to gender discrimination are removed and that women are on equal footing with men in every dimension of life. It cannot but be emphasized that this legislation protecting women's interests is most effective when it is complemented by efforts to empower women in all dimensions of their lives, as well as raising women's awareness of their rights in all contexts. Put differently, legal reform is not enough in and of itself: the status of women is not solely determined by law. All the resources of a country must be channelled into making gender equality a fact apart from law. The Women's Charter is but one form of protection for women's rights for ensuring their empowerment; there are many other forms of protection for women's rights in different arenas — all bearing equal importance in ensuring gender equality.

References

Leong, Sandra. "Feedback on Women's Charter: Making Defaulter's Pay". *Straits Times*, 1 November 2010, B1.

Polinsky, Mitchell A. and Steven Shavell. "The Economic Theory of Public Enforcement of Law", 1998. <http://www.law.harvard.edu/programs/olin_center/papers/pdf/235.pdf> (accessed 15 December 2009).

Sim, Melissa and Selina Lum, "Govt acts to ensure divorced men pay up", *Straits Times*, 14 September 2010, pp. AA1 and A6.

Singapore Council of Women's Organisations (SCWO). "Report on Forum on Enforcement of Maintenance Orders", 20 August 2009. <http://74.125.153.132search?q=cache:II8IIeORFgoJ:scwo.org.sg/wp/%3Fp%3D396+singapore+women%27s+charter+maintenance+orders+SCWO+

walter+woon&cd=1&hl=en&ct=clnk&gl=sg&client=
firefox-a> (accessed 5 December 2009).
Stivens, Maila. "(Re)framing Women's Rights Claims in
Malaysia". In *Malaysia: Islam, Society and Politics*, edited
by V. Hooker and N. Othman. Singapore: Institute of
Southeast Asian Studies, 2003.

Index

www.ingramcontent.com/pod-product-compliance
Lightning Source LLC
Chambersburg PA
CBHW032021020426
42338CB00002B/240